The New Way to Market for Manufacturing

Innovation That Grows Your Business

Bruce McDuffee

The New Way to Market for Manufacturing

Copyright © 2016 by Bruce McDuffee

ISBN-10: 0692645365
ISBN-13: 978-0692645369

This book is dedicated to my wonderful and supportive family:
Laurie, Ryan, Nicolas, Kaitlyn, Samuel, and Cassidy

Table of Contents

Introduction

What if I told you there was a way your manufacturing firm could increase annual growth rates to 10 percent, 20 percent, 30 percent, or even higher? Your firm can gain market share, get top-of-mind awareness (some would call this mindshare), increase credibility, and build a strong sense of reciprocity in the hearts of the people in your target audience. I am talking about the very people who will one day purchase a product like the one you are manufacturing. If you follow the framework presented in this book, you will achieve this position. Your manufacturing firm can be the go-to expert for the very problem your target audience faces. Your firm already has the expertise and the solution. All you have to do is stop pitching your products and start helping the people in your target audience be better, relieve a pain point, or enhance their passion, even if they do not buy your product today. When the day comes that these same people you have already been helping are ready to make a purchase, your firm will get the call first, and the business—even if you offer your product at a higher price than the competition. The value behind offering helpful, useful information can support a premium price in your market place.

This book was born out of frustration and opportunity. As a manufacturing marketer working for a global company, I was constantly frustrated by our leadership team's lack of understanding about marketing as a function and potential contributor to revenue. Because the leadership team did not understand marketing, they severely undervalued the marketing leader, team members, and our activities. Marketing was simply the people in the back, hunkered down in their cubicles making brochures, placing ads, setting up trade shows, and operating the company website. How could they not see the power of marketing as a strategic component of the revenue-generating machine?

After I was fired from that global marketing director job because I dared to challenge the status quo, I became a marketing consultant focused exclusively on the manufacturing sector. At last, I was free of the shackles forged by the corporation and its leaders who did not understand marketing. I was ready to make a killing as an independent consultant concentrating on the manufacturing industry. As I spoke to one manufacturing company after another, I realized that the lack of understanding and the associated severe undervaluation of marketing were endemic throughout the manufacturing sector. This consulting gig was not going to be easy. The vast majority of manufacturing companies seemed stuck in a time warp, a "Groundhog Day," if you prefer, where they conducted marketing as if it were still the late twentieth century. Many of the manufacturing leaders I spoke with not only did not understand or appreciate the marketing function, they also did not employ a marketing team. I recall talking to a CEO of a $2 billion-dollar company who told me he employed just six people in the marketing department.

My conclusion was and still is that marketing is undervalued and underutilized across the manufacturing sector. Further, I advocate that those manufacturing companies that can change their culture, along with the way they go to market, by advancing the marketing function to be a strategic component of the business will win in their space. Let me state this another way: those manufacturing companies that are willing and able to embrace marketing as a strategic revenue-generating function as I describe in the following pages will win in their market space with higher growth rates and higher market share. Those firms that do not understand the significance of a modern marketing function and continue to rely on the field sales team and/or the product team will lose share.

The mission of this book, along with the Manufacturing Marketing Institute (MMI), is to advance the practice of marketing throughout the manufacturing industry. Additionally, my mission is to help manufacturing marketing organizations and you, the marketer, learn about modern marketing strategy, tactics, skills, and technology.

Manufacturing marketing is very different from marketing in most other industries. By reading this book, you will learn about the extraordinary opportunity available to manufacturing companies. We will discuss marketing fundamentals and the importance of developing a proper marketing plan in order to establish a strong foundation critical to a viable revenue-generating marketing function.

One thing that is fairly consistent across most manufacturing companies is the strong product culture that overpowers nearly all other functions, except maybe the sales function. In Part 1, we will elaborate on the gigantic opportunity open to manufacturers who can embrace the New Way. In Part 2, we will look at the more formal practice of marketing. In Part 3, we will discuss how to overcome the product culture and advance a marketing strategy that does not wholly rely on product promotion. I advocate that manufacturing companies must stop pitching their products to gain engagement and awareness at the top of the funnel and replace product pitching with education that is not about the product. This is a tough sell in most manufacturing firms, and we will discuss how to address this cultural shift.

In Part 4, we will share specific tactics proven to be successful in making the shift to educational marketing as a fundamental strategy for growth. The primary tactic is launching an effective pilot program and gaining buy-in for a pilot. I have found that eating the product elephant one bite at a time is the only way to change the product culture. The first bite is a pilot program.

My ultimate vision for manufacturing companies is that they discard the industrial-age jargon and structure of having a sales team and a marketing team but never the twain shall meet. It is a rare thing indeed when a sales team is perfectly aligned with a marketing team. Instead, typically neither team understands or respects the other, but the sales team dominates. Marketing becomes the servant to the sales team and is at their beck and call for developing product-related content, much of it used only once and criticized as not effective.

In place of the traditional structure, I advocate for one revenue team under one leader. The various job functions may not be very different from the traditional structure, however, the concept is highly unifying. I firmly believe this is nirvana for manufacturing firms with a goal of increasing their organic growth rate by revising their go-to-market strategy.

Part I - The Gigantic Opportunity

"You can close more business in two months by becoming genuinely interested in other people than you can in two years by trying to get other people interested in you." —Dale Carnegie

Chapter 1 - The Hidden Expertise Within

Your manufacturing company is sitting on a gold mine. The gold lies just below the surface and is ever so easy to reach. Some would call it low-hanging fruit, ripe for the picking. The gold I'm talking about is the expertise of your own employees. Your engineers, product managers, R&D scientists, and salespeople all possess knowledge and skills that can solve myriad pain points for the people in your target audience.

The beauty of this opportunity is its simplicity. The people in your target audience are craving the very same information your employees possess. Think of it this way: your target audience has pain in their daily lives, and the expertise within your manufacturing organization is the ibuprofen for their pain. When you share this expertise, people will line up to listen. They will email, call, visit your website, and download your content. The best part is, when they are ready to buy what you and a slew of other companies around the globe are selling, your firm will get the call and the business because your company and your experts helped them to be better.

You will learn in the upcoming chapters exactly how to mine the gold of expertise to gain market share from your competitors who are not aware of their own gold mines. You'll learn how this expertise is not about the features and benefits of your product but about having a deeper and more meaningful understanding of the problems and challenges that plague a majority of the people in your target audience.

As an example of the gold mine of expertise, consider a medium-sized company that manufactures humidity measurement instruments. They manufacture high-end electronic devices that convert an electrical signal into an observable output. These devices are used by industrial manufacturers and pharmaceutical companies to ensure the quality of the production process and maintain quality during storage. In a search on www.globalspec.com for products and services related to humidity, we find 34,518 results as of this writing. In most cases, the products are perceived as a commodity by the potential buyers around the world. Most of the companies that manufacture humidity instruments will tout the product features and try to outmuscle the competition with field sales people or ecommerce.

One company decided to take a different approach. It decided to focus on the people in its target audience and the related pain points around making the measurement. The company found that there was a strong need or pain common to a majority of the audience: taking a measure of humidity is not easy. It is frustrating and challenging because most people do not understand how the sensor works to make the measurement. The marketing director started to mine the gold by uncovering hidden expertise throughout the company about the science of humidity. He found that if he could share the expertise of his scientists by teaching the people in his target audience about the science of humidity, the customers (and prospective customers) could make a better measurement. This made their lives better. When the day came that these same customers were ready to buy a humidity instrument, they called the company that helped them to be better.

That, my fellow manufacturing marketer, is how it's done. We will talk in depth about the details of why and how in the coming chapters.

Takeaway Actions:

1. Think about the expertise hidden among the scientists, salespeople, product managers, R&D groups, leadership, etc. in your company and make a list of specific people to seek out.
2. Start to informally discuss how the people on your list might share their expertise to alleviate pain points common to the folks in your target audience.

Chapter 2 - Culture of the Product

Most manufacturing companies have a very, very strong culture built around their products. This chapter will be counterintuitive to many if not most manufacturers reading this book. Read on and you will learn why you can grow your business and take market share by marketing without pitching your products.

Manufacturing companies that are able to stop pitching their products and start educating their target audience to gain awareness and engagement will win in their market space. Sharing expertise instead of pitching products is a far more effective means of marketing. This concept has been proven to work over and over in other industries and even in some manufacturing organizations. If used consistently, it is the secret to winning big in your market.

With direct A-B testing, I have compared product ads to educational ads many times. The education ad always, always wins by a huge margin. The largest difference I observed was in a GlobalSpec enewsletter ad. GlobalSpec is a media group that provides a global marketplace for industrial buyers. I ran a new-product promotion ad in the enewsletter. In the following month, I ran an educational ad offering a simple FAQ (frequently asked questions) document in the same position to the same audience. The ad offering the FAQ outperformed the new product ad by 800 percent. More specifically, the audience engaged with the new product ad 252 times and the FAQ ad 2288 times.

The fact is, the people in your target audience don't care about your product, your company, your CEO, or you. They care about what's in it for them. When they see your marketing message, they immediately ask themselves, "What's in it for me?" We all do this, either consciously or unconsciously. The answer comes quickly and is usually "Nothing is in it for me" as we move on by turning the page, deleting the email, ignoring the banner ad, etc. It doesn't matter how much you try to convince potential customers that the features of your product are good for them and superior to all other products on the market. The answer to WIIFM 99.9 percent of the time is "Nothing" or "Not enough."

To get a positive response to WIIFM, you have to prove to your target audience that you can help them relieve pain, be better at their professions, or improve their lives. One popular metaphor we can all relate to is dating and marriage. Leading with the product pitch is like trying to get a date by asking someone to marry you. Most of us know not to talk on a first date about marriage, the house we will someday live in together, or how beautiful our kids will be. Think of the top of the sales funnel as analogous to a first date. You need to show some interest in and goodwill toward your audience before they begin to care about your firm or your offering. An educational offer does that, providing value to the audience.

When someone in your target audience is faced with a problem and you offer a solution (without talking about your product), the answer to WIIFM is positive. They consume the content and relate a positive experience to your brand. With a product ad, unless your ad just happens to pass before the eyes of someone who is at that instant considering the purchase of your product type, there is nothing in it for them. This is why product ads perform so poorly. The percentage of people ready to buy the product at the exact instant they see the product ad is minute.

The problem and the opportunity lie in the culture of the product. In nearly all manufacturing companies, every aspect of the culture is centered on the product. Many firms have been building the same or similar products for 50, 100, or 150 years with great success up until a few years ago. Each and every employee loves that product. They understand that the only reason they have a job is because someone buys that product. They tell their friends and family about the wonderful product that is manufactured by their company. They attend meetings where everyone tries to come up with more reasons why people should want to buy that product. Their websites, brochures, and trade show booths tout the product. The power influencers within the company are those managers who own the product development, the employees who make the product, or the sales team who sells the product. Every other department is secondary, except marketing, which is even farther down the pecking order. In most manufacturing companies, the product rules, and any attempt to go to market without mentioning the product is perceived as ludicrous.

This is your opportunity. If you can change the culture within your company even just a little bit to focus on the people in the target audience and not your product, you're on your way to taking market share from those product-obsessed competitors. The people in your target audience are sick and tired of hearing about the product, the company, the CEO. The prospective customers think about themselves. They think about WIIFM. Use that to open a window of opportunity. Those manufacturing companies that can open their minds and move away from the product culture in order to help the people in their target audience will win.

You choose your target audience because you believe that someday they will buy what you are selling. If we look at the entire population, on any one day when they see your product ad, they will take action if they are at a very specific point that meets four criteria, called BANT: budget, authority, need, and time frame. Only a very small portion of the population (<1 percent) is aligned with your product pitch at the time they view the ad. Let's suppose 80 percent are faced with a problem that you can help them solve. On any given day, they are struggling with the problem. If you promote something like a webinar or a how-to paper that helps them address that problem, you have a much greater chance of them engaging with your asset and your brand. Perhaps 80 percent are interested in your knowledge content. Remember, we said that less than 1 percent are interested or ready to hear your product pitch at any given moment. The high level of engagement with your knowledge content leads to top-of-mind awareness and credibility as they get to know your company, brand, experts, etc. Then, when the day comes along and they have BANT, who do they think of? They think of the company that has been helping them relieve their pain. This is a huge competitive edge over your competitors who continue to simply pitch their products. That, my fellow manufacturing marketer, is the foundation of the new way to market.

Takeaway Actions:

1. Conduct an A/B test comparing a product ad to an ad offering only educational content. Make it a fair test and try your best with both ads. Make sure you pick a medium that can be conclusively measured. Keep the results ready for the time when you are ready to propose your pilot program.

2. Put yourself in the position of one of your prospective customers and ask yourself, "What's in it for me?" when you see a product ad as compared to an ad offering valuable content. Keep notes and confirm your hypothesis with primary research if you can get the budget and approval. This will be powerful data when you are ready to confront the strong product culture in your organization.

Chapter 3 - Sweet Spot of Engagement

Let's summarize what we have so far uncovered as the very big opportunities available to smart manufacturing firms. We have discovered that expertise is usually prevalent within any manufacturing organization. The expertise we want to mine is not the expertise used in building the product, but a deeper expertise around the underlying needs of the target audience.

We have an understanding that the best way to engage with the people in the target audience is by helping them relieve a pain point or enjoy a passion rather than pitching product features. In order to really understand the pain or passion points that can be addressed by sharing your firm's expertise, it's a good idea to conduct primary research in parallel with internal discussions with stakeholders. The collective assumptions or accepted knowledge about the target audience may indeed be inaccurate. I encourage you to put on your critical-thinking hat and question the collective wisdom that pervades most manufacturing organizations.

When choosing the sweet spot of engagement, it is important to collaborate with your stakeholders if at all possible. Doing this work as an individual or even as a singular marketing group is much less effective than collaborating in order to gain agreement and buy-in. The most common critical stakeholders are the sales and product leadership folks. If you are in a predicament in which your stakeholders dismiss marketing altogether, then you will have to go it alone, which I strongly encourage if the alternative is to do nothing.

The sweet spot of engagement is at the intersection of the pain or passion point you have identified for your target audience and the expertise you have uncovered among the employees within your manufacturing firm.

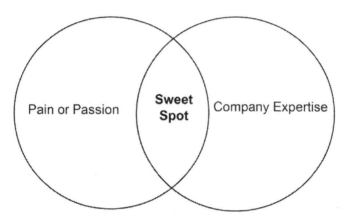

Sweet Spot of Engagement

The diagram above is meant to be a worksheet for brainstorming. You may come up with more than one pain point, expertise, or sweet spot, but it is important to choose only one of each for each business category. You may have more than one sweet spot of engagement, depending on the size of your firm and the structure of the organization. For example, you may determine a sweet spot for each product area or each business area. The sweet spot will define the topic or mission that will drive your marketing strategy, related tactics, and messaging going forward with the New Way to Market.

As an example, let us continue with the measurement instrument company we discussed in Chapter 1. One of the product groups in this company is humidity measurement instruments. After conducting primary research, the company discovered the pain point common to a large majority of the target audience is that humidity is a very difficult measurement to make consistently and reliably. Reliable and consistent measurement is critical to the target audience, which consists of pharmaceutical companies and semiconductor manufacturers. The related expertise, uncovered among the product engineers working in the research and development department, is their understanding of the science behind the properties of a moist gas (humidity). The sweet spot of audience engagement was agreed to be providing an education about humidity and humidity measurement technology to the people in the target audience who are frustrated by their inability to get a reliable measurement. The hypothesis is that by teaching them about the science, they will be equipped to make a better measurement.

Once you have determined the sweet spot and you have reached agreement with your stakeholders about the sweet spot, it is time to craft an audience-facing mission statement (AFMS). The AFMS will be your guiding light when it comes to making decisions about marketing activities and expenditure. If one of your colleagues suggests creating a piece of content or an activity that is not in line with the AFMS, it should be rejected.

As you proceed with building out your New Way marketing strategy with the AFMS as your compass, you will continually measure results to confirm your hypothesis. As with any hypothesis, if testing does not prove the hypothesis, you should go back to the drawing board and revise the sweet spot and the AFMS.

Continuing with our example of the humidity instrument company, the AFMS might sound something like this: "We help the people in our target audience make a more reliable, repeatable, and accurate measurement of humidity so that they produce higher quality goods in a more efficient manner."

Rather than calling it just a mission statement, I call it "audience-facing" for a very important reason. When most of us think about a mission statement, we think about the mission of the company. Many times these corporate mission statements sound like this: "Our mission is to be the preferred widget manufacturing company on the face of the planet." This statement is internal facing. I want to make a clear distinction between the corporate mission statement and the AFMS. It is important to notice the sweet spot of engagement and the AFMS are not about the product. They are about the people in the target audience. You will likely get pushback from your sales and product stakeholders around this idea. As you begin to collaborate, the product culture will kick in and you will hear that the expertise is in building widgets or creating new products. You must remain resolute and push them to see that the company's expertise goes much deeper than just manufacturing products.

Understanding the sweet spot of engagement and the AFMS contributes to the huge opportunity we are discussing. While your competitors build a strategy around pitching products, you will be mopping up the market share with broader and deeper engagement. A manufacturing marketing strategy built around an AFMS works wonders on the company's growth rate. I have personally developed such a strategy around this type of marketing pivot, moving from product focus to audience pain focus. My experience was in seeing growth increase from an annual rate of 3–5 percent to a rate between 20–25 percent within a two-year period. Naturally there is much more behind driving this type of growth beyond the sweet spot of engagement and the AFMS, which we will discuss more in Part 4, the how-to section. In Part 3 we will discuss more about how to overcome the product culture that is embedded deeply in most manufacturing companies.

Takeaway Actions:

1. Gather some trusted colleagues together for a preliminary discussion about your target audience's pain point and the company's expertise. Explain the ultimate objective of the AFMS. Depending on the tone and outcome of the preliminary meeting, you will get an idea about how strong the product culture is at your company. This preliminary meeting is a rehearsal for the main meeting with your stakeholders.

2. Prepare a research study to determine the pain points common to the people in your target audience. Use critical-thinking skills as you evaluate the collective knowledge about pain points that you will hear from the sales people and the product people. The combination of your internal assessment and your primary research will give you a good idea of the pain point. As you prepare your marketing research, keep in mind the expertise you have chosen. It may be the case that the primary research examines pain points in relation to more than one area of expertise.

3. Fill out the sweet spot diagram and craft your AFMS.

Chapter 4 - Globalization and the Internet

Most of us in manufacturing view globalization as the bane of the industry. Globalization means having to compete with other countries where cost of goods and cost of production are much less expensive than in the United States. Some would perceive globalization as forcing U.S. manufacturers to cut labor costs, cut profit margins, raise prices, or go out of business. Then there is the Internet, which seems to further erode profit margins by commoditizing nearly every product on the face of the Earth. It may seem like U.S. manufacturers have no choice but to either join in and offshore production or buckle down and slowly go out of business. Looking at it another way, the Internet and globalization have created a great opportunity for manufacturers that embrace the new way to go to market. Although very large corporations with a global footprint may seem to have an instant advantage because of their global infrastructure, the real potential is for small and medium-sized companies that can now compete for the very same customers served by the big guys. Yes, that is correct, if your firm is a small or medium sized manufacturing company, you can now compete around the globe and gain market share with the new way.

This is the silver lining for savvy manufacturers. Because of the Internet and globalization, you can engage and develop virtual relationships with the people in your target audiences like no other time in the history of commerce. For those manufacturing companies that remain stuck in the 1970s go-to-market paradigm, which includes maintaining expensive field sales people, trade show attendance, and product pitching (and there are a lot of you out there), without incorporating the new way, you will be forced to compete at the profit-margin level. Ultimately, you will have to reduce profit and cut expenses. Reducing profit and cutting expenses is the beginning of the death spiral for any manufacturing company. The choice is up to each and every company. You can watch profit decrease as you cut commissions to your sales team and reduce marketing spend (probably not in that order), or you can go all in with the new way and take market share from your laggardly competitors. Now is the time to act; the window of opportunity will eventually close because everyone will be up to speed with the new go-to-market strategy. I am assuming you are a smart manufacturer because you chose to read this book. Congratulations! You are about to start taking market share from the laggards.

The Amazon Effect is a big influence on the way we purchase a product. Amazon has raised the bar and changed expectations for how we expect to do business. Regardless of the purchase, we now expect to have easy access and transparent insight into the purchasing process, even if we are purchasing a multimillion-dollar piece of machinery for our factory. We expect to be able to log on to a convenient and intuitive website to monitor the delivery date of the product once we plunk down the money. We do not want to have to call, press a series of numbers, and leave a voice mail then an email to learn the status of our order. We expect to have instant easy access to the shipping route and timeline. We expect to be able to have access to payment options, reordering information, current stock, and above all, instant price comparison. This is the Amazon Effect and, like it or not, this effect is driving our expectations, even in the B2B manufacturing realm. The winners in your particular market space will be easy to do business with as benchmarked against the Amazon Effect.

Your opportunity, Mr. Smart Marketer, lies in the fact that your competition is playing the globalization game by competing on the features of the product, the company size, and/or the charisma of the CEO. This is a losing proposition because, as I stated in Chapter 2, nobody cares about your product, your company, or your CEO. They care about WIIFM. You can exploit WIIFM with the Internet, the great equalizer. No matter what you are manufacturing, ultimately a person is making the decision about what to purchase. It has been proven over and over that people make purchasing decisions based on emotion first, and they support the emotional decision with logic. The new way increases engagement well before a person starts to engage with your sales team. The new way exploits the Internet around the globe by creating virtual relationships before the other guys get the call.

Yes, pricing is important, but in all market research conducted over the past forty years, when buyers are asked to rank the top ten items that influence their purchase, price is never, I repeat never, the number one influence. If price is not the number one influence, then you may wonder what is at the top of the list. Usually it's people's trust or belief that their purchase will be safe. Once again, people purchase based on emotion and justify the decision with logic.

Globalization and the Internet enable the new way by sharing expertise to help the people in your target audience better relieve their pain, thus beginning a meaningful buyer–seller relationship. The Internet enables the savvy manufacturing marketer to start a conversation with a prospective customer anyplace on planet Earth. Remember, you do not start a conversation with a prospective customer by talking about your product; you start by talking about their pain and freely sharing your expertise to relieve that pain. This important step is conducted virtually, and you may or may not know your firm is creating these relationships, which will depend on how modern your marketing strategy, tactics, team, and tools have evolved to be.

While your competitors are beginning their engagement by talking about product features and ending up talking lowest price, you are winning the business by creating top-of-mind awareness (TOMA), credibility, and reciprocity among your global audience. Globalization and the Internet afford you the opportunity to reach more people, engage with a broader audience, and develop relationships twenty-four hours a day, seven days a week, 365 days a year, including while you sleep. The Internet and modern marketing tools are the keys to exploiting this opportunity. In Part 4, we will tell you exactly how to do it.

Takeaway Actions:

1. Assess the current state of the company. Examine the culture within your firm as it applies to globalization and the Internet. Are people in your company afraid, confused, excited, baffled, enthused? Have there been any concrete steps taken within the sales or marketing function to exploit the ability to connect virtually around the globe?

2. Assess how close your firm is to meeting the expectations created by the Amazon Effect. Is it easy to do business with your firm? Make a list of deficiencies and areas that can be improved.

Chapter 5 - Your Competition Are Laggards

Manufacturers, as a group, are laggards when it comes to marketing. Just to be clear, this is not meant to be a pejorative statement about manufacturers. The definition of the term laggard as listed in the Oxford English Dictionary is "A person who makes slow progress and falls behind others." The assertion that manufacturers are laggards with regard to marketing is an interesting phenomenon because manufacturers as a group are quite progressive when it comes to production, supply chain management, and new product development. However, when it comes to marketing, manufacturing organizations are laggards. Although I do not have any statistics, anecdotally, in speaking with hundreds of manufacturing marketers over the past several years, I've found that manufacturing is typically near the end of the line in adopting marketing technology, new marketing strategy and tactics, new marketing ideas, new marketing staff, or anything to do with marketing. This is your opportunity.

Because you are reading this book, I will assume you either are not a laggard or you do not want to continue being a laggard. Not to put too fine a point on it, I'll say it again, this is your opportunity. Your competition is probably not reading this book, because they are comfortable with being marketing laggards. They have justified in their own minds and socialized the idea that 3–5 percent organic growth is okay and it is simply the best they can do because of the globalization of the industry and the plague of the Internet commoditizing their product. Your competitors are sitting ducks. By applying the lessons in this book, you will take market share from your competitors. By the time they wake up and realize your business is growing by 10 percent, 20 percent, or 30 percent and mopping up market share, your firm will be so far ahead, the competitors will never catch up.

Suppose your competition is reading this book and is also getting excited about the possibilities of TOMA and broader engagement through helping the people in their target audience be better. That may well be the case. The winner will be the firm to apply the "new way" marketing strategy first. Let me repeat because this is a very important point. The winner will be the firm to get there first. The new way is like any innovation in business. Anything that works to gain a business advantage is quickly copied. The first movers gain the upper hand, but eventually the competitors catch up.

Some manufacturing companies will gain a vague understanding of the new way but will not quite be able to execute a new, fully functioning go-to-market strategy. They will not be able to cease and desist pitching products at the top of the sales funnel. A common symptom of a minimalist approach is in the ubiquitous white paper. Recognize that creating one piece of content like a white paper is not executing a strategy. In addition, in order to create a white paper that supports the new way strategy of high-level engagement, that white paper should not mention the product but should only offer helpful, useful information that relieves a pain common to the people in the target audience. A white paper created by a manufacturing company with only a vague understanding of the strategy will pretend to offer helpful, useful information, but it will be mainly about how the product features will alleviate the pain. These sorts of white papers mention their products over and over as the solution or the best technology. Your audience is very clever, and they'll see right through this type of faux knowledge marketing. In order to follow the new way, you have to be first and you have to execute the strategy purely. You cannot fake it because your audience will see it. Your competition faking it is your opportunity.

Another way your competition will miss the boat is in not socializing the concept behind the new way. The new way is not a six-month campaign. It is a cultural pivot away from product focus and self-centric marketing to freely sharing expertise with everyone in the target audience without pitching the product. Typically, when a manufacturing company does make the pivot and socialize the strategy, it takes twelve to eighteen months to see results on the top line. Many manufacturing firms will give up and write it off as a failed campaign after three to six months. The manufacturing firms that adopt the strategy and stick with it will win.

Sample Scenario #1: When no firms in your competitive space adopt the new way and everyone continues with the same old product-based marketing, this is the scenario: A person or a company in your target audience determines a need for the product you are all selling. The prospective customer does most of their self-education research via the Internet, and they talk to their peers either directly or via one of several social media channels. When they have collected enough information, they reluctantly engage with the sales team at several manufacturers that sell similar products. All of the websites are pretty much the same. All of the products are pretty much the same. (I know you don't like to hear this, but it is mostly true.) All delivery times are pretty much the same. What's left? You guessed it: price. There is always one company willing to drop their price just to get the business. All firms essentially lose a little piece of their corporate souls in this process as it plays out millions of times each week.

Sample Scenario #2: One firm (maybe your firm) has adopted the new way to go to market as they share knowledge and expertise with their target audience. This one firm has been publishing white papers, how-to notes, webinars, videos, etc. supporting a mission statement of helping the people in the target audience be better. None of the material mentions the product. As a prospective customer determines a need and begins to research their pain point, which can be relieved by the information and education offered by the firm, the helpful content shows up at the top of the search results in search after search. The prospective customer downloads white papers, attends webinars, and voraciously consumes a lot of other helpful content offered by only one firm among those companies that manufacture a similar product. Finally, the day comes around and the prospective customer has budget approval and they are ready to buy. The firm that has adopted the new way gets the first (and maybe the last) call. This firm has gained TOMA with this buyer. This firm has created an immense amount of credibility in this buyer's mind. The buyer has a strong feeling of wanting to reciprocate with the brand because of all the help the firm has provided. Of course, the buyer is obligated to get a few other price quotes from competitors. At this late stage, what does the competition have to offer? You got it: all they can offer is a lower price. The buyer is more than willing to pay a little more because credibility equals reliability and reciprocity is a powerful influence.

The new way to go to market creates TOMA, credibility, and reciprocity, which causes higher growth rates, bigger market share, and weaker competitors. The laggardly competition, which is unable and unwilling to change the way they go to market, is your opportunity.

Takeaway Actions:

1. Take a look at your competitors. Review their websites, trade show booths, brochures, and any other marketing collateral you can find. Are any of them using any resemblance of the new way? Try to recognize the various levels of competence in their go-to-market strategy and tactics. If no firms are executing on the new way, your window of opportunity is wide open. Be the first or, as the second, just be better.

2. Is your firm one of the laggards? Be honest and evaluate your current go-to-market strategy. If you determine your firm is not willing or able to adopt to modern marketing strategy, tactics and technology, you will need to decide if that is okay. If it is not okay, you have a lot of work to do. Read on to learn how to go from being a laggard to a powerhouse in your market space.

Chapter 6 - The Bad News Is the Good News

The bad news is that the global economy is not growing more than 2–3 percent each year. According to the latest United Nations Industrial Development Organization (UNIDO) World Manufacturing Production report for Q3 2015, overall manufacturing output is expected to grow at only about 2 percent year-over-year in 2015. All things being equal (absent implementing the new way marketing strategy), the best organic growth rate manufacturing firms can expect on average is between 2 percent and 3 percent. If you and your firm are satisfied with that growth rate, you may stop reading right now and stick with your tried-and-true go-to-market strategy. If you are looking for double-digit growth, read on my fellow manufacturing marketer.

The good news is that most or perhaps all of your competitors will settle for single-digit growth as the new normal for manufacturing companies. Most, if not all, of your competitors will not read this book and, even if they do, will not be able to stop their product-pitching ways. They will not believe that growth can increase by following the new go-to-market framework. Therein lies your opportunity. As I mentioned in the last chapter, the first movers will win market share. You can be the first mover. Very few manufacturing organizations will be able to change their culture from pitching products to sharing expertise. The firm that is able to embrace this new way to go to market will be able to grow their business by 10, 20, or 30 percent. Where will that growth come from? It will come from your competitor's market share. Now is the time to make the change. Opportunity is knocking for those firms that are able to embrace marketing as a source of revenue.

There is more good news. If you are a CEO or other executive in your manufacturing firm, you should understand that your marketers are smart. Unfortunately, your head marketer (CMO or VP of marketing) may not be as smart as the marketers who work for her. The marketers on the ground doing the work get it. They know about how to engage with a target audience by sharing expertise. Embrace your marketing professionals and let them be the kind of marketers they long to become. Encourage them to innovate, create, speculate, and experiment. Let them fail once in a while. You and your leadership team may be the very obstacle that is holding back your growth by not allowing your marketing function to advance and evolve into a revenue-generating machine.

You may be thinking that your marketing leader and her team do not get it. And, you might be right. If your team resembles a marketing function where folks work in the back cubicles chained up by a lack of faith and understanding in marketing, if they are still mainly setting up trade shows, making some brochures, and creating PowerPoint templates, then you are right. If that is your situation, use this book as a springboard to create and embrace a marketing leader and team who are revenue-generating machines. Yes, this means investing in the marketing function. It means finding a marketing leader who understands the strategic and tactical aspects of marketing, how that function can generate revenue, and how to discuss it with the executive leadership team. It means embracing a marketing team who knows how to use modern digital tools for engagement and measurement, a team who can drive revenue at ten times the rate of the field sales force and manufacturer's reps combined. It can be done and, in fact, it must to be done to win big. Marketers are smart, and they get it if you only listen to them once in a while.

The opportunity is astounding for manufacturing companies ready to reinvent their go-to-market strategy. Leaders often talk about innovation as a keystone to manufacturing success. Innovation applies to marketing more than any other function. Walk the walk when it comes to innovation. Most B2B manufacturing leaders consider innovation to be about new products or new processes within the production and distribution lines. There is no area today riper for exploiting innovation than marketing.

If you are a CEO reading this book, after you embrace marketing as a strategic function, let your marketers innovate and support that innovation. When the marketing leader comes to the next leadership meeting and requests funds for a strategy that does not pitch the product, give it to him! Listen to him with an open mind and an authentically innovative heart. Discard all of that old product culture baggage and try something new and innovative in marketing.

The bad news of the global economy is very good news for a manufacturing firm ready to make this change. You must be first in your market space because, as in all things in free-market capitalism, even innovative marketing will eventually equalize. Make hay while the sun shines and make the change to the new way in your go-to-market strategy.

Takeaway Actions:

1. As the chief executive, assess the state of your marketing leader and the marketing team. Ask them about the concepts raised in this book. Determine if they understand the opportunities we discussed throughout Part 1. If your marketing leader is not on board with these concepts, get one who does understand the idea and is able to put together a team to execute it. As chief executive, you really have two choices: you can ignore marketing and accept 2–3 percent annual growth rates, or you can advance your marketing team to become a strategic component of the business before your competition beats you to it.

2. As a marketer, prepare a presentation as if you were presenting a solution to your leadership team about how a modern marketing team can generate revenue better than any other function in the manufacturing organization. Sum up the opportunities presented in Part 1. This is worth doing even if you do not present it because it will prepare you for presenting your pilot program as discussed in Chapter 14.

Part II - Marketing as a Practice

"A goal without a plan is just a wish." —Antoine de Saint-Exupéry

Chapter 7 - The Marketing Plan

By my anecdotal estimation, only about 10 percent of manufacturing companies can put their hands on a proper, written marketing plan. You may be surprised to know that many chief marketing officers, owners, chief executive officers, managers, and directors are not embarrassed to say, "My marketing plan is in my head." Achieving success with the new way requires a proper, documented marketing plan. It's not the marketing plan itself that is so important, it's the decisions your organization is forced to make during the compilation of the marketing plan as well as the collaboration that is required to get everyone on the same page. The process of creating a proper marketing plan will include making decisions about the target market; positioning statement; value proposition; company strengths, weaknesses, opportunities, and threats (SWOT); competition; and much more. These decisions are your guiding light for your marketing strategy, tactics, tools, activities, and team members. The marketing plan provides powerful levers to use on the day you have to say no to the head of sales or head of product as they request (or demand) a new trade show in a market that was not in the marketing plan, for example.

I find it helpful to list the things that do not constitute a proper marketing plan. These are common elements within many manufacturing marketing departments' marketing plans but are not acceptable as a proper marketing plan:

- It is not an idea, wish, hope or concept in your head.
- It is not a spreadsheet with dates, activities, budget, etc.
- It is not an editorial calendar or social media calendar.
- It is not a list of campaigns.
- It is not a list of goals.

Each of the items above may be a single component of your overarching marketing plan, but even as a group, they will not suffice as a proper marketing plan.

Depending on the size and structure of your firm, it is entirely possible that you will have several marketing plans, with each individual plan based on geography, product family, or business segment, for example.

As an example of what not to do, let me tell you a brief story. I had just finished up my MBA and sat down to write my first marketing plan for an electronic instrument manufacturing company. I wrote a proper plan based on my own knowledge of the business segment for this particular firm. I proudly delivered my final document to the business segment director. She looked it over, smiled, offered a couple of complimentary platitudes, and placed it aside, never to be referred to again. It was a very good marketing plan, and I think it would have made a tremendous difference in the outcome of the business segment if the business segment managers had adopted it. My mistake was in not collaborating with my stakeholders as I developed the plan.

You must not write your marketing plan in a vacuum. In other words, you should not just sit down and write it on your own as I did for the electronic instrument company. It is important to have support from above and buy-in from your stakeholders. A marketing plan that is not a collaborative effort with agreement on the important decisions will not hold up when strategic decisions are being made about the direction of the business.

Before you delve into writing your plan, you must understand the components of the business. In order to understand the components, you need to assemble a diverse cross-functional team. I suggest some or all of these folks:

- CEO, president, or general manager
- Sales leadership
- R&D leadership
- CFO
- CMO

- Key members of your marketing team

Assuming you can get your stakeholders to participate, you need to be very clear about the expectations. All stakeholders should expect and understand that the marketing plan is an agreement between marketing and the other stakeholders. In essence, it is a contract defining how the business goes to market with the offering. Ensuring that all stakeholders understand the contractual nature of the marketing plan is very important because at some point after the work of the marketing plan is completed, one of your stakeholders will approach you or someone on your marketing team with a request, demand, or idea that is outside the scope of the plan that has been agreed to. The marketing plan is your supporting document when you have to say no. The marketing plan is the North Star, the guiding light, the compass for each and every marketing strategy, tactic, activity, tool, and team.

This is not to say the marketing plan will never be changed or modified; quite the contrary, it should be made clear that it is a dynamic, living document that will change from time to time. The changes should only come during planned review intervals, however, not on a whim. The expectations with your stakeholders should include the following considerations:

- The decisions reached about markets, positioning, value proposition, budget, measurement, etc. are agreements between the parties and will not be changed without further serious discussion.
- You will all agree to a regular interval for review and updates, usually six months at a minimum and two years at a maximum.
- The marketing plan is an agreement as to the strategy and tactics the marketing team will execute and the budget that will support the marketing function.

If your manufacturing company is one of those firms in which marketing is not respected as a strategic component of the business, it may be possible that you cannot get anyone to collaborate with you on your marketing plan. If that is your situation, my advice is to go ahead and create a marketing plan with your team. Try to gain agreement one by one with stakeholders, especially with the sales leaders and the product leaders.

The following is meant to be a summary of the components of a marketing plan and not a comprehensive guide for writing a proper marketing plan. There are many books written on this subject, and I encourage you to use one as a guide as you create your marketing plan.

Part 1: Assess the Current Situation

You must have a thorough understanding of your current situation. This is the step where you assess what the company thinks it is doing at the present. You cannot create an effective plan to move forward if you do not have a concise understanding of the point where you start. There are three sections in this step:

1. **Summarize Your Market.** This is where you bring in your cross-functional team for collaboration. The market summary should include a definition of market demographics, needs of your target market, trends, and current, past, and future growth. Michael Porter's five forces framework is an excellent tool for the market assessment. Keep in mind that understanding your market may require primary or secondary market research. A word of warning here: do not rely on the common or collective knowledge of your organization if you can avoid it. It is especially common for members of the sales team to think they are experts on the market situation. They are not. It is important to get input from the sales folks, but do not rely entirely on that information. The same thing goes for nearly everyone else in the organization. Do some research to support your assessment and understanding of your market.

2. **SWOT Analysis.** Prepare a summary of what you learned in the previous step using strengths, weaknesses,

opportunities, and threats (SWOT) framework. One common mistake I see in these summaries is marketers mixing up the strengths and weaknesses with the opportunities and threats. Strengths and weaknesses are internal to your firm and can be controlled. Opportunities and threats are external and cannot be controlled. It is important to be brutally honest when delineating the SWOT components. It is a good idea to designate someone to play the devil's advocate during these discussions.

3. **Analysis of Competition.** Include a SWOT analysis for each of your main competitors. It is important to understand your competitors' core competencies, value messaging, how the market perceives them, and why customers choose the competition instead of your firm. Again, you should use primary market research if possible, in addition to considering the collective knowledge of the people within your organization. As mentioned above, beware of collective knowledge as it is often exaggerated or even downright wrong.

Part 2: Set Objectives and Identify Critical Issues

In this next step you will be setting objectives for the marketing function and identifying issues that are already apparent or may become apparent as obstacles to achieving the objectives. Objectives will come from the higher-level business mission, strategy, and goals. Business objectives may center on growth, maintenance, or profitability. Each of these drive different marketing objectives.

For example, growth could drive marketing objectives such as increase market share, promote a diversified offering to multiple target markets, or develop more products. Increasing profitability may drive marketing objectives such as increasing efficiency of marketing activities and improving ROI of marketing tactics. It's important to tap the senior managers who agreed to participate in the marketing planning process at this point to ensure the marketing plan's objectives are aligned with the business objectives.

As with any proper objective, the marketing objectives must be specific, measurable, and have a deadline. The objectives should be realistic, and the marketing team must believe the objectives can be achieved. Ideally, there should be an incentive plan in place to encourage individuals to strive to reach the objectives. Some examples of specific objectives:

- Grow the number of customers by 25 percent by the end of the fiscal year.
- Increase revenue from existing customers by 30 percent in two years.
- Reach breakeven by end of the fiscal year.
- Participate in three community events during the next twelve months.
- Ensure average ROI on marketing activities of at least 75 percent.
- Contribute 25 percent of qualified leads to the sales funnel each quarter.

One important objective that should be in every marketing plan but is often overlooked is support of internal marketing. It is very important that all internal stakeholders are aware of the critical strategic and tactical marketing plans. The marketing team should be promoting things such as the positioning statement, value proposition, messaging, marketing objectives, tactics, activities, results, and other issues. Internal marketing helps align the entire revenue team to the objectives, resulting in a very powerful execution of the plan.

The second part of this section is to identify problems or critical issues. If there are issues that may prevent achieving the objectives or activities that must occur to ensure the successful execution of the plan, they should be identified. For example, if achieving ROI of 75 percent is an objective, a critical issue may be that it will be necessary to purchase a marketing automation platform to measure and report ROI results.

Part 3: Perform Target Market Analysis

It is impossible to have an action plan without knowing your target. Suppose someone handed you a bow and arrows and told you to go ahead and hit the bull's-eye. You accept what appears to be a highly sophisticated compound bow with a set of precision arrows, but there is no target. The person who gave you the bow continues, "Go ahead, just shoot the arrow and hit the target." With no target in sight, how will you ever succeed? This little metaphor mirrors what happens in business more frequently than you may believe. It might sound something like this: "Here is your marketing budget. 'Everyone' is our target market. Now go ahead and get us some brand awareness, good leads, and grow the business."

A target market of "everyone" or "all industries" is the same thing as having no target at all. Even companies like Pepsi and McDonald's define a target market that is not "everyone."

It is imperative to identify your target market so you can use your resources efficiently and effectively. Markets may be defined in terms of geography, industry, business or consumer, sex, age, income, etc. Choosing a target market is also referred to as segmenting the market. Your decisions should be based on a combination of feedback from internal stakeholders who have a direct dialogue with the target audience and market research. It is a big mistake to omit input from either.

Target market analysis should be completed with an open mind and should be reviewed on a regular basis. The final result should be communicated throughout the company. This decision (choosing a target market) will drive the marketing strategy, positioning, messaging, and marketing activity.

One last note: It is important to consider where or if the people in your chosen target market congregate to share information. There must be an efficient way to reach your target audience with your message. If a majority of the target market does not congregate virtually or physically, it will be very expensive and most inefficient to get your message in front of them. In the manufacturing world, industry associations are a good example of a place where the people in your target market congregate and share information. A trade association offers numerous venues where you can reach a large group in your target audience in one instance. They may get together at the annual industry trade show, read the trade journal, regularly visit the association's website, and subscribe to email newsletters.

Part 4: The Marketing Strategy

At this point, you should have a good understanding of the business situation and associated marketing situation. You should have a clear understanding of the business objectives and critical issues that exist and their effect on the marketing plan going forward. Your target market should be clearly defined and you should have a consummate understanding of the value your firm brings to the target market.

The marketing strategy is where you bring in the famous "Four Ps of the Marketing Mix." As a quick refresher, the four Ps are product, pricing, place (channel), and promotion. This section covers the first three Ps. The fourth P, promotion, will be discussed in Part 5.

The product strategy depicts the existing product line and future product roadmap as aligned with the overarching business strategy. The product strategy should describe how each product fits the positioning statement and supports the value proposition. Product marketing strategy can become very complex in a short time. I strongly recommend you work with your product managers and business leaders on this section.

The pricing strategy must also align with the positioning statement and the value proposition. For example, if you position your brand as high value with premium pricing, you should not worry about winning business by offering the lowest price. It takes a very different infrastructure to compete on low price than it does to compete based on a differentiated product offering. It also helps to specifically define the pricing strategy as premium pricing, penetration pricing, economy pricing, or a skimming strategy.

Place describes the go-to-market sales channel. This strategy describes how the product you manufacture is offered to the end user. Your firm may offer the product only through resellers or manufacturer's reps, through direct sales, or some combination. This decision goes hand in hand with the other four Ps, especially pricing. Should you make the decision to use distributors or resellers, your gross margin requirement may be different than if you choose to sell via a direct-sales force. This decision also affects your marketing programs, which we will discuss next.

Part 5: Marketing Programs

Promotion is where most marketers hit their sweet spot. Most marketers love creating and designing programs. Some love the excitement of the measurement. Others believe you have not lived until you experience hitting the Send button and watching how many people click through the email or fill out the form. Promotion is the culmination of the previous four steps.

As you begin to build your promotion plan, it is critically important to remember your analysis, results, and agreements up to this point. Promotion should be designed for the target audience using the positioning statement and value proposition as well as the agreed-upon business strategy and marketing strategy. The promotions should support the objectives you have previously agreed to with your stakeholders. A promotion plan designed to generate leads is different from a plan designed to position the brand through thought leaders in the space, for example.

The promotion plan will include some of these tactics: print advertising, digital advertising, direct mail, public relations outreach, search engine optimization (SEO), search engine marketing (SEM), direct sales promotion, direct marketing, etc. Naturally, you have a limited budget and limited resources and it is important to keep those limitations in mind. The most effective promotion plans include both outbound activities and inbound activities integrated around the same message. It is very important to ensure the promotions support the strategy and objectives. Marketers are a lively bunch, and once the ideas start flowing, it's easy to lose focus in the excitement. Tactics agreed to in the promotion plan should be measureable if at all possible.

Part 6: Financial Plans

This is the section where manufacturing marketers tend to demur. After all, this is the sandbox where the big boys and girls play and talk about things like net this and gross that. Why should the marketer get involved or even begin to try to understand this stuff? Because for marketing to make a difference and a contribution to the manufacturing business beyond creating ads and setting up trade shows, the marketer has to understand the financial language, speak the language, and demonstrate how marketing is directly contributing revenue.

Your ultimate goal should be to transform the internal perception of marketing from a cost center to a business builder and revenue engine. To achieve this goal, marketing must understand the financial metrics and understand exactly how they affect those metrics. Until you are able to have this conversation with the C-suite, it will be very difficult to change the perception that marketing is merely a cost center.

There are three parts to the financial plans section of the marketing plan: financial metrics, forecasting, and budget for expenditure.

Financial metrics come from your CFO. It is beneficial to include some company financial data to help justify and compare the forecast and the marketing budget/contribution. The financial metrics section should include a reference to the latest income statement, cash flow statement, and balance sheet. Targets or key performance indicators (KPIs) such as sales revenue growth; earnings before interest, taxes, depreciation, and amortization (EBITDA); and gross margin should be specified in the marketing plan.

Forecasting is usually a joint exercise with other key stakeholders. The forecast should be based on data and not just on someone's best guess. The sales forecast may also drive the marketing expenditure in some cases. The forecast can be broken up into myriad types: market or segment sales, product sales, cost of sales, and/or channel.

The most commonly known financial metric for most marketers is the budget for expenditure. In my experience, most manufacturing marketing teams get handed a budget number they have little control over. Unfortunately, a culture that treats marketing like a child being handed an allowance is all too common and deadly to the marketing function, which is striving to advance the practice of marketing to become a strategic component of the business and having a seat at the leadership table. Accepting your marketing "allowance" only cements the marketing function position as a cost center ready to be cut at a moment's notice.

As a first step toward changing the negative perception of marketing at your firm, I suggest negotiating for a budget linked to the revenue goals. This single step will elevate the importance and the contribution of marketing. I suggest including a projection for the marketing contribution to business objectives and tying the expenditure to these contribution numbers. For example, include the percent contribution to revenue, percent contribution to new sales opportunities, and percent contribution to closed business in the forecast portion of the financial plans section. Use net contribution as a foundational measure of the effectiveness of marketing. Avoid talking about "cost per" metrics with your stakeholders, and especially with the C-suite. Instead, talk about "revenue per" metrics. It is important to know the "cost per" metrics, but I suggest keeping that data within the marketing team. This not-so-subtle change helps further position the marketing function as a producer of revenue, not as a line item on the expense ledger.

Net contribution is a strong indicator of the effectiveness and efficiency of the marketing function. The formula listed below is, essentially, a ratio of the gross margin less the cost of the revenue function and the revenue generated. Although one could argue it is not a true contribution, it is an indicator and you can watch the trend as a performance indicator of the revenue team.

Net Contribution (%) = [(Sales Revenue – COGS) – (Cost of Sales and Marketing)] / Sales Revenue

You will still need to plan your marketing spend, but that is something most marketers already know how to do, so I won't delve into that any more than to say it should be included as part of the marketing plan.

Part 7: Measurement and Control

What good is all this thought and effort if you don't know how well it's working? Thus the need for measurement. The old saying "What gets measured gets done" is true for marketing. The marketing plan is typically constructed during a relatively short period of time. The macro as well as the micro environments are going to change. In this modern era of lightning-speed flow of information and globalization, I think we can all agree that conditions change on a regular basis. Therefore, marketers must be continuously assessing the environment and comparing our marketing activity results using some type of measurement process.

The first step in measurement and control is to gain agreement with your stakeholders on the metrics themselves. These metrics are sometimes called key performance indicators (KPIs). There are hundreds of metrics you can choose from. Tools such as marketing automation platforms and web analytic tools enable many different kinds of measurements. Some of the more common metrics used to evaluate a marketing plan include page views, conversions, leads, clicks, click-through rate, open rate, form completion rate, etc. Financial-related metrics may include profit, revenue, net contribution, or pipeline contribution.

The point I would like to make above all else when it comes to metrics is that the KPIs you choose will send a strong message to the C-suite executives. The message may even be subliminal, making it even more important (or more dangerous). If you choose your KPIs around marketing-speak such as CTRs, page views, open rates, likes or retweets or if you choose your KPIs around cost or expense language such as cost per lead, cost per attendee, or cost per form, you are positioning yourself and your entire marketing team as "those folks down the hall who do our ads, maintain the website, and make our brochures." That is not necessarily a bad thing, until the company decides to cut costs. Many times in a manufacturing company, marketing is the first thing to be cut. C-suite meetings will always have someone who suggests, "Surely the company can do with less marketing since they (the marketers) are always talking about obscure metrics and cost of this or that." Without proof that marketing brings in revenue, executives perceive marketing as a necessary expense (read: evil) but don't appreciate the value of marketing to the business. If your company executives feel this way and you do not like it, it is your own fault. Start talking revenue and stop talking cost. Stop talking about marketing metrics outside of the marketing team. If you want marketing to be perceived as a strategic asset and a partner at the business leadership table, *make your metrics about revenue*!

In order to implement proper measurement and control, you must have the proper tools in place to capture the critical data you have agreed to measure. It does not do any good to agree on measuring sales pipeline contribution if you are not able to easily capture the data. You should be able to capture and document closed-loop reporting in order to report meaningful metrics. There are hundreds of tools available. Some of the more popular and proven tools are Marketo, HubSpot, Salesforce, and Google Analytics, to name a few.

John Wanamaker, an early proponent of marketing as a way to grow business, coined a famous saying back in the late 1800s: "Half the money I spend on advertising is wasted; the trouble is I don't know which half." With a proper measurement system, you will know what is working and what is wasted, allowing you to make adjustments to optimize your resources.

Part 8: Executive Summary

The executive summary is written last, but is placed in the front of the document. Do not try to write the executive summary first, before you put the work in on the entire document. The executive summary should outline a compelling argument and hypothesis that is supported by the data in your marketing plan. Tell the reader why your plan will support achievement of the business goals. Tell it straight, no spin. If you did your job with each of the seven steps, writing the executive summary will be natural and easy.

There are two main purposes for writing a marketing plan:
1. To define, clarify, and agree on your marketing strategy and tactics
2. To convey information to stakeholders

If you are presenting your hard work to an investor or senior executive from whom you desire buy-in and/or support, they will likely only read the executive summary before scanning the rest of the marketing plan. You may be thinking to yourself, "Why should I go through the time and effort to write a proper, comprehensive marketing plan when all I really need is a one- or two-page summary?" See number one above.

If you consider yourself a professional marketer, you must write your marketing plan. If you think you are a professional marketer and you do not have a written marketing plan, then, Sir or Madam, you are no professional marketer. It is well worth the time investment. It is good for your business, your career, and your reputation.

Takeaway Actions:

1. Find out if your manufacturing company possesses a written marketing plan. Ask key leaders where you can find the marketing plan. You may find out there is no plan. In most cases, you will be provided with a spreadsheet or slide deck that is in the category

defined above as not a proper marketing plan. If you are in one of those rare companies that already has a proper, up-to-date marketing plan, rejoice and study the existing plan.

2. If your firm does not have a proper marketing plan, get started and write one using the guidance above along with a textbook as a guide. If you are the marketing leader, it will be easier to initiate this project than if you are lower down the hierarchy. Even if you are lower down the hierarchy, it is a great learning experience to write your own plan. Although writing a marketing plan on your own is the last resort, do not rule it out completely.

Chapter 8 - Engagement versus Shouting

As humans living in the modern age, we are being shouted at during nearly all of our waking hours. I am equating shouting to interruption advertising. TV commercials, Internet ads, billboards, magazine ads, telemarketing calls, unsolicited email, et al. These methods of marketing or advertising interrupt whatever it is you are doing when the ad shows up. We have all become experts at filtering and tuning out these messages. Shouting or interruption marketing can work if you are able to shout the loudest. The loudest shouter must also spend the most money. This is how Oracle became the powerhouse in ERP software, by shouting over and over again that they were the best. In the old days, when broadcast television was only one of a few advertising channels available, manufacturing companies like Maytag and GE shouted their messages over and over, year after year as they interrupted our enjoyment of a favorite TV show. Maytag got us all to believe that it was the most reliable brand when it comes to washers and dryers by showing us the lonely and bored Maytag repairman. GE shouted their message "GE brings good things to life." Many of us who grew up in the '60s, '70s, and '80s are still influenced by these types of interruption, shouting messages that still live in our minds.

If your manufacturing firm has a huge marketing budget, shouting or interruption marketing might be a viable option. For the rest of us, we must get engagement with our target audience by offering value in a normal voice or even a whisper. To illustrate the difference, consider your daily battle with your email inbox. Picture a useful email you look forward to receiving each day, week, or month. You opted in because you like the email. When you receive the email, you gladly click on it and peruse the offer or the helpful information. It is relevant, so you do not mind receiving that particular email. This is engagement marketing. Other examples of engagement marketing are a podcast you listen to regularly because you find it entertaining, useful, or both. A webinar you registered to view and attended is another form of engagement. Any type of subscription is a reaction to engagement marketing.

It should be noted at this point that an effective go-to-market strategy most likely includes a combination of push and pull marketing, a.k.a. shouting and engagement marketing. The difference is that the push marketing, or shouting, conducted with the "new way" strategy promotes the educational content and not the product itself.

The difference between shouting and engagement is in the offer. Shouting talks about the company or its product. The vast majority of people on the receiving end of shouting or interruption marketing just do not care. In many cases, we form a negative perception of brands that use this type of marketing. Engagement marketing offers something of value to the people in the target audience. The value helps people in the target audience relieve a pain point or fan a passion. This value builds credibility and top-of-mind awareness. As humans, we are willing to engage with a brand, an advertisement, or a person who offers us a gift such as the value of relieving a pain. We feel a strong urge to reciprocate, and in the case of business, reciprocity manifests in a purchase.

For the remainder of this book, we will focus on engagement marketing. Engagement marketing takes longer to gain traction but ultimately increases the growth rate of a manufacturing firm several times over interruption marketing. Sales lead quality is much higher with engagement marketing as compared to interruption marketing. Engagement marketing creates more satisfied customers and drives positive word of mouth as industry colleagues compare notes about the various firms offering certain products and which ones are offering helpful information.

Now let us discuss a strategy for engagement with your target audience.

Takeaway Actions:

1. Assess your current marketing activity. Are you shouting and interrupting the people in your target audience with product ads? Are your emails relevant to your audience or are they about your company and your product?

2. Take a look at your last email or your home webpage. Count up all the first-person pronouns. If you count a lot of words such as we, our, us, etc., you are probably shouting and not engaging.

Chapter 9 - The Two-Stage Funnel

Within the manufacturing buyer process, there are really only two stages to the ubiquitous sales funnel. The top of the funnel is where you market to engage with (or gain attention from) the people in the target audience. As mentioned in Chapter 3, by determining the sweet spot of engagement, you introduce your brand and offering to the target audience using educational content that helps the people in your target audience relieve a pain, fan a passion, or just be better in their day-to-day professional activities.

When those same people in your target audience are ready to buy the thing you manufacture, they drop down to the bottom of the funnel, where you tell them about your product and your company. Just before they are ready to make the purchase, they want and need to know about the details of your product, features, and the firm itself. If you have been successful at the top of the funnel and your competition is not better than you at engagement, you will get the business as long as your product lives up to expectations.

What about the middle of the funnel? You cannot map the buyer's journey to the middle because there is not a common path between the top and the bottom. Therefore, I am proposing that the sales funnel for most manufacturing companies has only two parts, engagement at the top and product information at the bottom. What happens in between the top and bottom is not predictable nor is it controllable. In many cases, people will bounce around in the funnel, moving from top to bottom then back to the top. Most manufacturing companies are very strong at the bottom of the funnel.

The fundamental problem with the old go-to-market strategy is in trying to engage with the people in the target audience who are not ready to buy when they see your first message that pitches products. It does not work anymore. The basic premise of the new way is using knowledge-based content in the engagement phase. Most manufacturing companies are still using the old way, and they are perplexed as to why they cannot grow their businesses. Be the early adopter, and you will win.

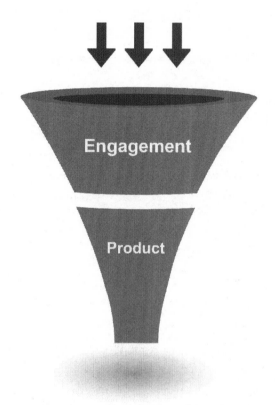

The 'New Way' Sales Funnel Has No Middle.

As mentioned in Chapter 1, engagement is where you can take advantage of the big opportunity that exists right now within most manufacturing market spaces. The firm that does the best job in engaging with the people in the target audience will win. In the minds of your target audience, the factory that produces the product is inconsequential. Your product looks just like your competitor's product. Trying to differentiate the product during the engagement phase is a waste of time. Save that for the bottom-of-the-funnel interactions. The product does not matter and the company does not matter during the top-of-the-funnel engagement phase of your relationship with a new prospective customer.

The secret to success for engagement lies in a thorough understanding of the pain that is common to the people in your target audience and the expertise that resides within your firm that can help relieve that pain and make their lives better. You may recognize this statement as the definition of the sweet spot of engagement we discussed earlier. Helpful information or education shared freely with the people in your target audience sets your firm apart from all of your competitors that are still pitching their products at the top of the funnel. Successful engagement positions your brand top-of-mind with your audience. Your brand gains a higher level of credibility than your competition because your firm is positioned as the expert in relieving this particular pain point. The information and education you share is a gift. Offering a gift evokes a desire in your audience to reciprocate. Reciprocity manifests in a purchase from your firm and not your competitor.

TOMA + Credibility + Reciprocity = Higher Growth Rates, Larger Market Share, and Higher Profits

At the top-of-the-funnel stage of engagement, you must not propose that your product is the solution to their pain. Save that idea for the bottom of the funnel. Your expertise around the product, not the product itself, is what they want to hear about. Here are a few examples to illustrate the idea:

If your firm manufactures particle measuring instruments for clean rooms, the expertise you may want to share is explaining the different classes of particle measurement and how they relate to different classes of clean rooms. Or you might teach the folks in your target audience about the regulatory environment for pharmaceutical clean room operation.

If your firm manufactures paper air navigation charts or tablet apps, for higher engagement teach the people in your target audience how to read a VFR chart on paper and/or in the tablet app. You teach them how to be a better pilot by helping them to be more proficient with airplane navigation.

If your firm manufactures irrigation equipment for industrial farms, share your expertise about efficient irrigation of large farms so they can be more profitable by being more efficient with irrigation.

It takes more than just one offer to earn TOMA, credibility, and reciprocity. Your engagement strategy must be ongoing, have a regular cadence, and be consistent in supporting the engagement mission. The process of regular touch points is called nurturing. Nurturing is defined in dictionary.com as "to support and encourage, as during the period of training or development; to foster." The primary assumption is that your engagement strategy is aimed at those people who do not know your firm or have forgotten about your firm. By nurturing them with a regular dose of helpful information, you are building a powerful relationship so that when the day comes around (assuming you have chosen your target audience well) and these people whom you have been nurturing are ready, willing, and able to buy the product you manufacture, you will get the call and you will usually get the business. That is why engagement grows market share, increases growth rates, and improves profitability.

Takeaway Actions:

1. Has your marketing department defined the buyer's journey in multiple stages? Determine if it is accurate and useful. If not, propose the simplified two-stage funnel.
2. Determine how your competition is attempting to engage with the audience. Chances are they are pitching products at the top and at

the bottom of the funnel. This is your big chance. Read on to learn how to take advantage of your product-pitching competitors.

Chapter 10 - Where Does Product Fit?

As I have stated throughout the book, those manufacturing companies that can stop pitching their products will win market share. What I mean is that manufacturing companies should not introduce themselves by talking about the product. As mentioned in the last chapter, the product plays a very important role in the practice of marketing, and that role lies at the bottom of the funnel, after the firm has earned TOMA, credibility, and reciprocity during the top of the funnel engagement phase (where we never pitch products).

Product marketing is important to the successful completion of the purchasing process. In many manufacturing companies, product marketing has nothing to do with the marketing function, but is more about product development. Typical activities a person on the so-called product marketing team may perform include research and development of new and existing products, market research to determine the product development roadmap, and creating product literature such as specification sheets and user manuals. They usually view the marketing team as the people who do their bidding in creating ads, brochure layout, spec sheet layout, webpage updates, etc. Many product marketers come from the engineering side or the sales side of the business. Rarely does a person with the title product marketing manager have a strong academic or practical background in marketing.

I suggest eliminating the term product marketing in favor of product development to avoid confusion between the two very different functions. Product development is a source of information for the marketing function, and marketing could be a source of information for product development, but they should remain separate and disparate functions. Having said that, it is also very important for the product development group to work very closely with the marketing group. Their success is intertwined. Product marketers are product developers. They require information from the market, but they are not marketers.

They know very little about strategic marketing and even less about tactical marketing. They are great at product development.

If you give a product marketer a chance to promote their product, they will talk about the product ad nauseam with little effect on top-of-the-funnel engagement. If you tell a product marketer you want to promote their product line without talking about the product, you will be summarily dismissed. I suggest letting them do what they do best, which is developing the product line and turn over the marketing to the professional marketers.

This next paragraph might sound antithetical to the thesis of the new way and it is subtle in that making a connection to the brand and the offering is not the same thing as directly pitching the product and company. However, during the engagement stage (top of the sales funnel), it is still critically important to connect the brand and the offering to the useful content. It can be a delicate balance between not pitching the product but making sure the consumer of your educational content knows who is helping them, what they offer, and how to reach them when the time comes. It does not help grow your revenue if you fail to make this vital connection. We will discuss the how-to in more detail in Part 4, but for now, let us stipulate that the connection between helpful and useful content and the brand and the offering must be made and made strongly without pitching the product. Do not pitch the product or the company, but do make the connection.

The people in your target audience get it. They know you ultimately want to sell them something. That is why most manufacturing firms are in business. It is very important to let them know what you manufacture in conjunction with providing them with helpful content. Many times, the connection to the brand and the offering can just sound like a short commercial. As an example, if you are producing an educational webinar, the moderator can make a brief statement about the sponsor of the webinar before diving in to the educational content. The slides should be presented on a branded template and, perhaps at the end of the webinar, the moderator can remind the audience once more about the brand, the value proposition, and how to contact the firm should they want to know more about the products. At the same time, there is no mention of the product during the meat of the presentation.

The product pitch is a critical part of the purchasing process at the bottom of the funnel. Information about the product features and benefits must be potent, easy to find, and compelling. The information must be easily available when the prospective customer is ready to move into the bottom of the funnel and make the purchase.

In summary, I want to be clear about the fundamental tenet of the new way to market, i.e., not pitching the product. I do not mean stop pitching the product completely. That would be preposterous. When a prospective customer is ready to buy and reaches out to engage with your sales process, pitch that product! When you are introducing your company and your brand at the top of the funnel, before they know your brand or after they have forgotten about your brand, do not pitch products! Once again, at the top of the funnel share expertise and educate the people about something that matters to them.

Takeaway Actions:

1. Take a look at your own firm. Does it have employees with the title product marketing? If yes, are they experience in marketing strategy and tactical execution? Assess who is making the strategic marketing decisions in your firm. Is the current structure of your firm's product department optimal or is it strangling the growth rate?

2. Prepare your presentation that goes along with the "stop pitching products" strategy. Be clear about the need for strong product pitching at the bottom of the funnel. Be clear about the need to stop pitching products at the top of the funnel.

Chapter 11 - Where Does Sales Fit?

I n most manufacturing companies, the belief is that the sales team generates the revenue. The sales team may be a direct-sales force, a network of manufacturer's reps, or some combination. The salespeople are the heroes because they bring home the bacon. The power of influence within a manufacturing company usually resides with the sales team, the product team, or some combination of the two. It is extremely rare for the power of influence to reside with the marketing team.

The marketing team, if one exists at all within the manufacturing organization, is relegated to being the service center for the sales team and the product group. In other words, the marketing team produces whatever the sales team and product group demands. Their contribution may include producing and creating brochures and presentation slides, attending trade shows, creating seminars and webinars, overseeing social media posts, and doing nearly anything under the sun that is desired by the sales team.

As a manufacturing marketing consultant, I worked with a company structured as I just described in the previous paragraph. The marketing department acted as a vending machine of collateral for the sales team and the engineering (product) team. This story is representative of the challenge facing manufacturing marketers around the world as they try to reconcile how the sales team fits with the practice of marketing. This particular manufacturing marketing team wanted to advance to become an effective, modern marketing team that participated in generating revenue through proper lead generation strategy and execution, content marketing, and marketing automation. As with most marketing organizations, they had a limited budget, people, and resources. Head of marketing was a title tacked onto the vice president of engineering's title. No doubt he was a brilliant engineer, but he was completely clueless about the practice of marketing. Just the fact that he was appointed to lead the marketing team tells you where the leadership at this particular multibillion-dollar global manufacturing company placed the importance of marketing.

I was invited to attend their annual marketing planning meeting. The marketers were smart and good at marketing. They presented what they were asked to present. At the end of the meeting, the vice president of engineering/marketing told them he was disappointed. Imagine how they must have felt. I guarantee you that each and every marketer was completely demotivated, and some were just plain pissed off. To top it off, the vice president told these professional marketers they should demonstrate more "pizzazz" and "flamboyance." Needless to say, the professional marketers in the group were confused by this directive. How disheartening.

In preparation for their huge annual trade show, the sales leader told the marketing leader that sales wanted a laser light show at the trade show. The particular laser show they wanted would cost in excess of $150,000. The marketing lead gave the sales team a choice between the laser light show and a lead generation program backed by high-quality content. The sales team chose the laser light show as a clear message at this company that sales matters and marketing does not matter.

Although this is a sad story, it is not atypical. It is the nature of manufacturing to undervalue the marketing function.

Does sales have a place in the practice of marketing? Not in the traditional manufacturing company. If I may be so bold, I suggest that sales should be one part of the marketing function and the leader of the sales and marketing group should be a marketing professional. To take this dream even further, I have a vision I would like to share with you, dear reader. Consider a manufacturing company where the structure is such that there is no sales department and there is no marketing department. In its place is a revenue team under the leadership of a seasoned marketing and sales professional who is not only a consummate leader, but is also a technology aficionado. Within this revenue team, the roles would be defined according to how they contribute to generating revenue. Possible roles would include:

- Customer care
- Field liaison
- New business
- Creativity and innovation
- Customer support
- Technology operations

If you look closely, you will notice that these roles are a mix of what were once known as sales and marketing roles. The personnel would also be integrated physically within the office space, if possible. They would strive to achieve the same goals and objectives as one team. Leadership would be unified and treated evenly, regardless of the role. Unifying the old sales and marketing roles and eliminating the old-school jargon would go a long way toward aligning these different parts of the revenue-generation engine. What better industry to build a structure called a revenue team than the industry that makes things?

Part 5 is dedicated to a full discussion about the concept of one revenue team.

Takeaway Actions:

1. Determine how the sales and marketing functions are perceived at your company. Is sales perceived as the revenue-producing group and marketing perceived as the subservient, expensive brochure-creating group? It might be hard to get an honest answer, but be persistent. Ask your senior leadership if you get a chance.
2. If you like the idea of one revenue team led by a marketing professional, write down a vision for your company. Describe the details of the group mission, job descriptions, hierarchy, numbers, etc.

Chapter 12 - Where Does Technology Fit?

The practice of marketing in the modern age requires modern technology. You may rightfully question this assertion, especially if your manufacturing marketing team is still operating with spreadsheets and other relatively antiquated technology. The reason modern technology is essential for the new way to go to market is because people do not go through the purchasing process (or the buyer's journey, if you prefer), in the same way we did even five years ago. The people in your target audience go through the same purchasing process you do and we all do. We start out with an Internet search using Google, Bing, or Yahoo. We gather information from various websites that show up high in organic search results or from ads that show up on the search engine results page (SERP). We check in with colleagues, family, and friends via social media or old-fashioned conversation. We check for any online reviews or negative reports and finally end up contacting a few companies that offer similar products. As a final step, we contact a few companies that offer what appear to be extremely similar products.

Note that the final step is contacting a few companies directly after all the research and self-education is completed. This is a critically important point. The manufacturing firm that has been providing useful and helpful content during the investigation phase has established a relationship with the prospective customer well before that prospective customer contacts the company. The helpful company has established TOMA, demonstrated credibility, and evoked a sense of reciprocity with the person before the other companies even get a look from the consumer. The company that gets the call out of the blue and has not been practicing the new way has only one option, which is to offer a lower price. If one of your competitors is offering helpful content during the customer's investigation via the Internet and you are not, you will probably not get the business, even with a lower price.

Modern marketing technology is the apparatus that enables engagement during the investigation phase of the customer's buying journey.

Many manufacturing companies still operate their sales and marketing departments as if the Internet did not exist. Yes, most have a website, but these days a website is table stakes. Many manufacturing firms depend on a field sales team that pitches products in reaction to a direct inquiry or a tip from a trusted confidant. As we depicted in the paragraphs above, by the time the field sales person reacts to an inquiry, the firm operating in the new way has already established a relationship through TOMA, credibility, and reciprocity.

Do you see the problem? Your prospective customers are buying like it is 2016, but most manufacturing companies' marketing and sales technology is from the late 1990s. You cannot operate a modern marketing function able to capitalize on the new way without marketing technology.

I fondly remember my younger days, when I was a bag-toting salesman traveling all over the country peddling my employer's products in the early 1990s. My company sent me to a sales training class put on by a franchise called Sandler Sales Institute. Dave Sandler founded the business, which used to be based on a selling method built around the idea that the salesman held the power of information and the prospective customer did not have access to this important information. The buyer needed the salesman's knowledge about the industry, new technology, competitors' choices, and pricing. Sandler taught us to use this leverage to gain commitments from the buyer and to forge a bond with the buyer to facilitate a perception of trust and reliability. The buyer's purchasing process involved contacting the vendor about 15 percent of the way through the purchasing process. This gave the salesman and the company a lot of room to build a personal relationship with the customer. In most cases, the salesman whose personality was the best fit for the prospective customer got the business. Some salespeople still try to operate in this manner, but they will fail if they do not adapt.

In 2016, most research shows that prospective customers do not contact your sales team until they are 70 percent or more through the purchasing process. Without modern technology, you have no idea who has a need for your product until they have nearly made their final decision. All things being equal (in other words, assuming no one is offering helpful content virtually), the decision comes down to price, and we all know how fighting for the lowest price works out for business. Not too good.

The Internet is now the primary source of information for individuals and companies during the early phases of the buying cycle. One could argue that the function of a field sales professional is heading toward extinction. For example, we as buyers are able to scan a bar code with our iPhones and immediately know pricing and availability around the globe. We are able to go to Yelp and instantly see reviews about a certain restaurant we are considering. We can search with Google, MSN, Yahoo, etc. and find a white paper about any and all technical topics. We can immediately post about our satisfaction or dissatisfaction with a product, service, or company on Facebook, where we have potential access to more than 1 billion people around the world!

If your firm is going to adopt the new way, you must embrace technology. You cannot engage with your prospective customers while they are in the self-education phase without modern marketing technology. Specifically, this is the technology you must have to convert to the new way:

1. **An Interactive, Up-to-Date Website.** I'm not talking about a 1990s website with a bunch of outdated, static pages. You need a content management system (CMS) behind your website, built with the visitor in mind. You should include a blog, complemented by a subscription-based enewsletter. The site must be intuitive, easy to navigate, and offer a useful and valuable experience to the visitor. WordPress is probably the most prevalent and easy-to-use CMS for manufacturing companies. Your website is the main place where you engage

with your target audience while they do their self-education. If your site is offering valuable content and your competitor is not, you get the TOMA, credibility, and reciprocity, which means you will likely get the business.

2. **A Customer Relationship Management (CRM) System.** A CRM is essential for a few different reasons. First, this is your database of record for customers and prospective customers. Yes, I understand most companies have a database for accounting purposes, but you must have one for sales and marketing purposes. Salesforce.com is probably the most prevalent CRM in manufacturing. If you are one of those companies where your sales folks keep their own super-secret spreadsheet of customers and prospective customers, please, please stop that practice and get a proper CRM. That one step alone will launch your business into a higher growth rate. Ultimately, when you have a modern revenue-producing marketing function in place, you will want to be able to track marketing spend and return on investment. You will need a CRM that tracks opportunities to close in order to accomplish a return on investment for marketing spend.

3. **An Email Service Provider (ESP).** The major tool you will use to engage with your target audience is email. Do not use Microsoft Outlook as your email tool. Outlook is great for one-on-one communicating, but it is not equipped for mass email sending and tracking. If you use it that way, you will damage your email reputation and end up on a slew of blacklists that prevent your emails from getting through firewalls. An email service provider is specifically designed for email marketing. It has built-in safeguards and manages your unsubscribe list and bounce lists. Some of the more popular ESPs are Constant Contact, MailChimp, and Emma.

4. **A Marketing Automation Platform (MAP).** Marketing automation includes email marketing as one component of a greater set of marketing tools. Other features included with a

MAP are landing page design and hosting, website visitor reporting, lead form creation, lead management, ROI reporting, and more. If you are new to modern marketing, you should start off with an ESP and as your marketing team matures, move into a MAP. Marketing automation is a powerful tool, but it should not be adopted on a whim. Some of the more popular MAPs are Marketo, HubSpot, Oracle Marketing Cloud, Act-on and Salesforce Marketing Cloud.

There are thousands of different marketing technology offers to choose from. One word of caution: avoid the shiny new object syndrome. It is wise to remember that a piece of technology or a new tool will never solve your problems by itself. All tools require a strategy for implementation and use, a way to measure results, and at least one super-user who owns and loves the technology. The marketing team leader and the team culture should be conducive to adopting and integrating technology into the team and the strategy. If you think your team is not willing or able to embrace technology, you need to look at the team composition first.

Takeaway Actions:

1. Audit your current technology status. Look for a CRM, MAP, ESP, and other tools. If you are lacking any of these tools, determine where the customer database and the prospective customer database reside. Do you have access to one, both, or none?

2. As you lay the groundwork for the new way, be aware of what new tools you will need to bring on board and the requirements for implementation of such tools. Depending on the structure of your firm, it could be easy, hard, or next to impossible to implement a platform such as a MAP. If you fall into the category of "next to impossible," do not give up. We will talk about how to deal with strong cultures in Part 3.

Part III - Culture of the Product

"Your customers don't care about you. They don't care about your product or service. They care about themselves, their dreams, their goals. Now, they will care much more if you help them reach their goals, and to do that, you must understand their goals, as well as their needs and deepest desires."

—Steve Jobs

Chapter 13 - The Culture of the Product

This is my hypothesis about why the culture of the product is so strong in manufacturing companies. When manufacturing was in its glory days during the post–World War II boom, there was really no need for marketing as we know it today. Marketing activity consisted of some print ads and trade shows. The product was king, and all the manufacturing company had to do was invent and/or produce a product and people would buy it if they had the money. There was high demand and limited supply, so if your product was adequate, customers would buy it. If a product person or a sales manager decided they wanted to run an ad, it was usually a seat-of-the-pants decision, and the nearest administrator was tasked with putting together an ad based on a sketch on the back of a napkin. There was no strategy or coherent plan in place to move product except for the sales team, an occasional advertisement, and the regular trade show.

Surely, how smart do you have to be to put together a trade show? was the thinking in the typical manufacturing company back in the 20th century. So it was an administrative task and not the responsibility of a professional business person. We can clearly see how the manufacturing culture was beginning to define the role of marketing as an administrative function in support of the sales and product teams. This culture strongly persists today. The sales team is usually well funded with fat travel expense support and high compensation. In fact, the sales team is so revered in some manufacturing companies that only the C-suite receives higher compensation. On the other side, there is the marketing team, with minimal salaries, usually no bonuses or commissions, and budgets that are the first to get cut when sales revenue drops.

It is perfectly natural for a manufacturing company to grow up cultivating a strong product culture. After all, the company exists to make the product and sell it for more than it costs to produce. The perception is that the product is everything. If that product is not purchased, there is no profit, and if there is no profit, there is no company and ultimately no jobs. The logical conclusion is simply that the product is everything. As the company grows up, all decisions are based on the product. People are hired because of their expertise with some aspect of the product. How could any culture other than a strong product culture exist at a manufacturing company?

Cultures do not change easily. Peter Drucker famously stated, "Culture eats strategy for breakfast," meaning a new strategy does not have much of a chance against a culture. This is especially relevant when it comes to a product culture. The culture in most manufacturing companies is dominated by either the sales organization or the product/R&D organization, or both. The CEO is usually from product management or operations. Once in a while the CEO comes up through the sales ranks. It is very rare to see a CEO who comes from a functional marketing background. The only chance a strategy has against a culture is if the CEO drives that strategy home over the long term.

If we assume my hypothesis about how and why the culture of the product exists and is so strong within manufacturing companies, we ask the question "How can marketing assert itself as anything more than an administrative function?"

The answer is to be proactive and demonstrate results with a pilot program around a specific tactic that can show the power of a new way strategy. You will likely not get permission from sales or product management to do something different. They do not want marketing to be any more than it already is within the corporate structure. Collaboration, offering ideas in meetings, or talking about new ways to market will fall on deaf ears. This is all because of the unflappable culture of the product.

My experience has been consistent with the statements above. When the power centers are sales and/or product management, marketing does not have a chance. If we stipulate that the perception of marketing is that it is an administrative function, why not just do something different then tell your stakeholders about the success?

Here are a few ideas:

- Set up and broadcast an educational webinar. It takes some hours, and you should have the support of your manager, but the success will be obvious if you choose a topic relevant to your target audience. Do not try a webinar about one of your products. I guarantee it will fail and fail miserably.

- Set up an enewsletter with a theme that resonates with your target audience. The enewsletter should not be full of news about your company and your products, it should he focused on one piece of useful information for your readers. The enewsletter should be opt-in only.

- Create a new frequently asked questions (FAQ) paper. These are pretty easy to create, and you can promote it for free in your social channels. Again, do not do an FAQ about your company or one of your products. Make the FAQ topic relevant to a pain point common in your target audience.

We will talk more about how to kick off an official pilot program that gets your marketing foot in the door of a product culture in the next chapter. The point to take for now is that culture is difficult to overcome, so you will need to be clever and go around the existing culture to get a few quick wins as you chip away at the strong culture of the product.

Takeaway Actions:

1. Test just how strong the product culture is at your company by examining the background of the C-suite executives. Do any of them have a functional marketing background? In your next meeting with the sales team or the product team, propose a

marketing activity that does not touch the product and see what happens.

2. Talk to the sales and product leaders to assess their perception of marketing. Do they consider marketing as subservient to the demands of sales and product management? Do they respect or even understand marketing as a contributor to the organization?

Chapter 14 - The Magic of a Pilot Program

As mentioned in the last chapter, sometimes you just have to go ahead and do something different, then share the amazing results. The level of risk depends on your organization and the level of control your department and the other departments want to have over the organization. In some high-control organizations, you could get fired for going rogue. In other organizations, where the culture supports new ideas, you could be lauded and promoted for doing something innovative. You will have to decide how far to push the envelope in your organization. I suggest that if your innovation is perceived as going rogue and defying the powers that be, you would be better off working for another company.

There is a more formal way to approach the introduction of the new way in the face of a strong product culture. Suggest a pilot program. Chances are high that you can get support and funding for any type of pilot program that highlights innovation, even if that innovation comes from the marketing department. What manufacturing company does not like to think of itself as innovative? If you offer an innovative idea in support of company growth or other business goals, you will get approval. The reason pilot programs are magical and why they are almost always accepted is because they are perceived as not permanent and non-threatening. Conversely, if you were to propose a complete change of the existing go-to-market strategy, chances are slim that you would be able to overcome the product culture. Therefore, I suggest you use the pilot program to get your "new way" foot in the door. If you are the chief marketing officer with a seat at the leadership table, you might have a chance at revamping the strategy all at once. If you are a close advisor to the CEO and were brought in to turn around the marketing and sales teams, you have a good chance of revamping the strategy. If you are like most of the manufacturing marketers in the manufacturing industry, with little power or influence but a lot of passion, the pilot program is the best way to go.

There are six steps to creating a pilot program designed to demonstrate the power of the new way and the power of sharing expertise for free as a means to engage with the people in the target audience.

Step 1: Write down your goals and objectives. If the goal is to demonstrate the power of knowledge-based marketing as a way to generate engagement, then you should clearly state that goal and how the results will support the goal.

Step 2: Gain commitment from a subject matter expert to support your pilot program.

Step 3: Choose the particular tactic you will propose. I strongly suggest choosing a tactic that allows you to show real, verifiable numbers. An educational webinar series is a great choice because you can easily show the number of registrants and attendees along with critical data about each person. You could argue that your webinar pilot program will deliver qualified leads.

Step 4: Identify and procure the tools, develop the content, set milestones, select a launch date, and execute.

Step 5: Share the results and be prepared to show how the results demonstrate proof of your hypothesis.

Step 6: Ask for resources and support for an extension of your original pilot or request a second pilot program to further demonstrate the concept of the new way.

If your first pilot program is successful, you will likely be allowed to do a second pilot. Eventually, the pilot programs will merge together and you will have achieved your initial desire to pivot the marketing strategy from product pitching to sharing knowledge and educating the people in your target audience.

Takeaway Actions:

1. Keep in mind the politics of your organization as you craft your pilot program. Unfortunately, in some organizations the success of new ideas is feared and they are treated as a threat rather than an opportunity. Form good alliances and collaborate as much as possible. Avoid conducting your pilot program as a stealth activity. Your chances of achieving the ultimate goal of transforming the go-to-market strategy are better with collaboration and transparency.

2. Be patient, but be persistent. You might consider treating your marketing position and the firm where you reside as a laboratory where you can experiment in a real-life environment. Treating your company as a laboratory allows you to learn the lessons of success and failure, which will go a long way toward forging a successful marketing career.

Chapter 15 - Shout from the Hilltops

"All you need in this life is ignorance and confidence, and then success is sure." —*Mark Twain*

I f it is your desire to change the way your manufacturing company goes to market, then you will need to let everyone know about your pilot program successes. I will warn you in advance, it will not be easy. People generally do not like change. Some people will be jealous of your success and work behind the scenes to undermine it. Others will point out all the flaws in the idea or declare loudly that the success was a fluke. I'm sure your idea will be fantastic, but you will find a lot of resistance when you try to introduce a marketing strategy that does not pitch the product. Even your own boss might be against the idea and, depending on the character of your boss, she may not be completely supportive of your efforts behind closed doors with her peers and superiors. It takes guts, determination, and persistence to change the culture of the product and introduce a new way to go to market. On the positive side, you may just make a name for yourself and earn a promotion or, maybe even better, a higher-level position at another company.

My first pilot program, which eventually evolved into a go-to-market strategy pivot, was a live educational seminar. I was the marketing manager for a company that manufactured measurement instruments. It was a strong product culture. The product managers held the profit and loss responsibility, and they ruled with an iron fist. My direct boss was a bit more open minded than the product kings, and he was interested in trying out new ideas. He supported me in developing a seminar program that educated the people in our target audience about the science behind the measurement and about the parameter, with no mention of products as part of the educational material. There was very strong resistance from the sales team. They ridiculed the idea and claimed no one would even show up. The product bosses at the headquarters also ridiculed the idea because it did not promote their products. They had a very self-centered view about their products and failed to really understand the challenges and pain points common in their target audiences. Yes, indeed, the product force was strong in this company.

With the support of my direct manager, I went ahead with the seminar idea. Interestingly, in a company filled with highly educated scientists, no one was willing to step up as the subject matter expert and speaker, so I made myself the expert based on my engineering degree, self-education, and field experience with the measurement applications.

The results were beyond my wildest expectations. I sent out one email invitation. In those days, the registrations came in via fax. Within twenty-four hours of sending the invitation, I had more than thirty-five people registered. I readily admit I was not a polished speaker and the material was a little rough around the edges, but the reviews from the attendees were very positive—enough so that I planned three more seminars over the next few months. I was lucky enough to have a good boss who continued to support the effort in spite of the derision I believe he received from the product bosses overseas. The ridicule continued for more than a year, in spite of continued successful seminars. Eventually, the seminars became accepted and adopted as a standard inclusion to the annual marketing strategy. Some of those who ridiculed the seminars became strong supporters when the sales leads increased and the growth rate started to increase. I made sure to let people know about the success of the seminars. I did "shout from the hilltops" about this new way to engage with the target audience by helping them to be better at their profession.

This second story occurred a few years later. Once again, I was facing a strong product culture and would have to overcome the resistance to a new go-to-market idea. As technology was improving around broadcasting through the Internet, I proposed the idea of educational webinars. Recalling my experience with the live seminars, I knew what I would be up against. I learned that it is hard to buck the status quo of the product culture at a manufacturing company. I knew it would be hard to introduce new ideas to an old company. I also learned that sometimes you just have to push through the resistance and go ahead with your idea. Naturally, I learned that I would need support from at least one friendly higher-up and, fortunately, at this new company I controlled my own marketing budget.

I had started as a brand-new marketing manager at this global measurement instrument company, and they were struggling, with growth numbers in the single digits. It was a traditional manufacturing company where the product was king and sales was queen. Product managers had the profit and loss responsibility and, therefore, the power and influence. Further, guess what, the product managers were at the corporate headquarters in Finland, of all places. I didn't even know where Finland was on the globe. Not only was I faced with a strong product culture, I was faced with a completely foreign corporate culture and a foreign culture in general.

I was eager to put my newly minted MBA in marketing to good use. I was and still am a big advocate of lifelong learning and professional development. I had read about webinars and how some thought leaders in the marketing space were using webinars as an education tool to engage with the people in their target audience. Keep in mind this was more than ten years ago when the term content marketing was just emerging and the technology to produce your own webinar was available but just in the early adoption stage.

I remember the day quite well. It was a gray and rainy Monday morning when we got "the speech" from the general manager. "The speech" was usually meant to be a combination of inspiration and fear, causing motivation and trepidation. This one was no different. The bottom line message was that the company was losing market share and everyone needed to pitch in and work harder because the bosses in Finland were on her case for more cash flow.

I was young and I was inspired. I went into the general manager's office and pitched my idea about using a webinar to educate the folks who were in our old Lotus Notes database about something that mattered to them as a way to get more leads and fill the sales funnel. She said, "You mean teach them about our product?" I said, "No, we'll teach them how to be more effective whether they buy our product or not. That way we'll get TOMA." She said, "What the hell is TOMA?" I explained that TOMA stood for top-of-mind awareness and it is the key to long-term and robust growth. She laughed and she laughed and then kicked me out of her office, claiming she had more important things to do and that I should focus on my next postcard design for the quarterly direct mail campaign.

Needless to say, I was less inspired, but I believed in my idea and I believed in the concept of education as a way to engage with the audience and grow a business. Undaunted, I proceeded to visit the U.S. product manager to pitch my idea about educational webinars. His response was "We tried webinars and they don't work." He went on to explain that the product team tried webinars on two separate occasions to launch new products and only a couple of people signed up; therefore, the conclusion was made that webinars do not work. I tried to explain to him that people do not really care about the products. Naturally, as the product manager, he was appalled and personally offended. I said, "They don't care about the product or the company, they care about WIIFM." He said, "What the hell is WIFFM?" I explained that it means "What's in it for me?" from the audience perspective, not from the company perspective. He laughed, but it was more of a good-natured laugh than a mean and dismissive laugh. He told me to go ahead and put this educational webinar together, and he agreed to fund it as a pilot program.

I was very excited and reenergized. In spite of the derisive looks I got from the leadership, salespeople, and even my own marketing peers, I put it together. When I had everything ready, I sent out an email invitation to our database of about 10,000 customers and prospective customers. One day after the email invitation hit the inbox, about 200 people registered! Ultimately, approximately 500 people registered for that first webinar! The laughing had stopped. The country manager now wanted to know more about this idea of educational webinars. We even had some notice from the executive team in Finland. It seems that getting the company in front of 500 people from the target audience to spend an hour with your experts at a cost of about $2 per registrant is an impressive feat.

I expanded that webinar program from one to a series of eight educational webinars. The business grew at a rate of more than 20 percent per year over the next few years. Was the growth all due to webinars? At that time, we did not have the tools to prove it, but I suspect most of the growth was because of TOMA, credibility, and reciprocity created by the webinars. The pilot webinar program was the beginning of the strategic shift to what I now call the new way to go to market.

When you have success with your pilot program, you need to shout it from the hilltops, metaphorically speaking. The shouting should not in a boasting or arrogant fashion, but should be in a practical and one-on-one discussion, demonstrating the results in as tangible a way as possible and explaining the direction you are heading with your new way to go to market. Be sure to talk the language of the person or group whom you are addressing. When you talk to the C-suite, you must talk the language of the C-suite.

Takeaway Action:

1. As you prepare your pilot program, include a plan to share the anticipated success of the program. You might include one-on-one conversations, group presentations, lunch and learn presentations, announcements in the internal company newsletter, postings on the company intranet, etc. Communicating the success in a smart and relevant fashion will be critical to introducing the new way strategy.

Chapter 16 - Learn to Talk the C-Suite Talk

According to a study performed by the Fournaise Marketing Group in July of 2012, 80 percent of CEOs do not trust marketers and are not impressed by the work done by marketers. In comparison, 91 percent of CEOs do trust their CIOs and CFOs. Ouch! The number one reason given for not trusting marketers is that marketers are too disconnected from the financial realities of the company.

There are two major contributing factors at play. One factor is that the C-suite does not understand marketing beyond being on the receiving end of advertising. Only about one in five CEOs has a background in marketing. The leaders who occupy the seats at the leadership table such as the CFO, COO, and CIO rarely have any background or education in marketing. In many cases, their marketing acumen boils down to how they, as human beings, perceive the marketing they are exposed to. Sadly, in many cases, they like what they like based on their own socialization and not because of any practical or analytical reasons. When they personally like some type of marketing they are exposed to, they believe it must be good marketing. This was definitely the case for the VP of engineering/marketing I mentioned in Chapter 11 who wanted more pizzazz and flamboyance. These are typical comments from a senior executive who knows nothing about marketing.

The second contributing factor is the marketers themselves and how they present themselves to the leadership and the organization. As marketers, it is our collective fault that most CEOs of manufacturing firms do not understand marketing. If your CEO is a good leader, then he is usually fair and a good listener. He listens to what his head marketer tells him and draws conclusions about how the marketing function contributes to the organization. If we, as manufacturing marketers, talk about click-through rates, open rates, downloads, likes, etc., we will not gain respect much less a seat at the leadership table. The language of the C-suite is about moving product, top line, and bottom line.

According to the new way, it is our job to talk to the C-suite about the benefits of the new way. The benefits we discuss must be about the goals and pain points of the executives if the language is to resonate. We must educate the C-suite about marketing in this modern age, where the very people in our target audience who will one day purchase what we manufacture are self-educating and making as much as 70 percent of their purchasing decisions before ever contacting our firm. We must educate the C-suite about why we need to help the people in our target audience be better and relieve pain points, even if they never become a customer. We must talk about how TOMA, credibility, and reciprocity combine to grow revenue by taking market share from the competitors.

Use the data from your pilot program to talk about how marketing has contributed to the sales pipeline. Do not, under any circumstances, talk about marketing metrics such as click-through rates, open rates, likes, shares, retweets, etc. Nobody cares about those metrics except marketers. That is not to say they are not important metrics because they are important, but only to marketers. I guarantee if you tell your CEO that you have 70,000 likes on your company Facebook page, he will dismiss that information immediately. However, if you tell him that marketing campaigns contributed to 35 percent of the new sales opportunities in the pipeline this month, he will take notice and may engage in further conversation. If that happens, you have just taken a step toward advancing the marketing function so that it plays a strategic role within your company. Below are some examples of C-suite terms and Marketing Team language to ensure a clear understanding of the value you wish to portray to each of the different groups.

C-Suite Language:

Net Contribution (Net$_c$): This is the best measure of effectiveness. Do not mistake net contribution for an absolute return on marketing investment (ROMI). Net$_c$ is a perfect measure of efficiency because it is a percentage based on the gross profit. The trend tells the C-suite how the overall strategy and tactics are driving revenue.

Net$_c$ (%) = [(Sales Revenue - COGS) - (Cost of Sales + Marketing)] / [Sales Revenue]

Marketing Contribution to New Opportunities: Expressed as a percentage. Again, not an absolute measure, but useful as a month-to-month benchmark. Good for talking points with the executive team. Be ready to explain how you derive the number.

Marketing Contribution to Closed/Won Opportunities: Expressed as a percentage. A great benchmark that proves marketing is contributing to revenue. Look for trends. Could also be correlated with other specific marketing metrics such as impressions, emails sent, etc. to indicate the general effectiveness of the marketing activities.

Revenue per Marketing Qualified Lead (MQL): Always couch your stakeholder-facing metrics as revenue as compared to cost. Think about how your CEO or CFO perceives the marketing function based on reporting revenue per lead as compared to cost per lead.

Number of MQLs: The net number of leads passed to sales is, of course, an important measure of success for the marketing strategy and tactics. Be careful about reporting on the funnel points to the C-suite, as they will be more bottom-of-the-funnel (revenue) oriented and may not care about the leads at the top of the funnel. Whether or not you discuss the sales pipeline or sales funnel depends on how marketing-savvy your conversation partner seems to be.

Although I mentioned this earlier, it is worth mentioning again. Never, never talk about "cost per" anything with the leadership team. Using this phrase cements an idea that is likely already in their minds— that marketing is a cost and not a source of revenue. Always, always talk about "revenue per" or "contribution" with the C-suite, with the objective of creating the perception that the marketing function is a source of revenue.

Marketing Team–Only Language:

Cost per Click (CPC): This is the best measure to compare any of the myriad marketing digital activities to each other. You should establish a benchmark for an effective ad spend. After a while, you'll be able to reject marketing activities that do not meet your benchmark and do more of those that meet or exceed your benchmark.

Cost per Thousand Exposures (CPM): This is a good measure to determine reach. As with CPC, you should establish a benchmark for this metric. Cost per click and cost per thousand exposures should be considered together when evaluating the results of activities and determining if you should continue or discontinue certain tactics.

Click-Through Rate (CTR): Another good benchmark for comparing the effectiveness of materials and venues. The CPC, CPM, and CTR together help the marketer make decisions about effectiveness.

Funnel Conversion Metrics: Marketing qualified leads (MQL) to sales accepted leads (SAL) to sales qualified opportunities (SQO) to closed/won opportunities and other relevant conversions are important to allow you to pinpoint problem areas. These metrics are often discussed with the sales team.

Revenue and Cost per Attendee: These are good specifics for evaluating the effectiveness of events such as trade shows, conferences, or seminars. Be cautious of making binding decisions based only on these metrics. There are likely to be intangibles that should be considered, such as the salesperson's opportunity to see multiple customers and prospects in a short span of time at a trade show.

Once again, as a rule of thumb, only use the "cost per" metrics within your marketing team to help evaluate effectiveness of your marketing activities. As already mentioned, never ever talk "cost per" with the executive team.

I will share a story to illustrate this point. I once attended a global marketing meeting at a company where I was a marketing manager. The CMO was going over the metrics for the past year. One metric she was particularly proud of was that the team had sent out around 1 million emails globally over the past year. The session that followed her KPI analysis was a Q&A with the CEO. As the CMO was proudly telling him about the 1 million emails, you could see his eyes glaze over. He did not care if the marketing team sent out 100 emails or 10 million emails; he cared about how marketing contributed to revenue. She persisted in talking about "cost per" metrics with the CEO. After several other questions and answers, the CEO was about to leave the room when the CMO once again brought up the 1 million emails. The CEO paused, did a half turn, and smiling, said, "Next year your number is 2 million." Enough said.

Takeaway Actions:

1. Define your current KPIs or general reporting metrics. Are they mostly "cost per" metrics and marketing metrics that mean nothing

to anyone outside of the marketing team? Determine which metrics are being reported to the C-suite. Are these metrics couched in the C-suite language or marketing speak?

2. If your metrics are not defined, define them as presented above with one set for C-suite discussions and one set for internal marketing benchmarking. If you are the marketing leader, teach your team how to speak the C-suite language and encourage them to share the C-suite metrics broadly around the company. Remind them to keep the marketing "cost per" metrics internal to the marketing team. Make a concerted effort to build a perception of the marketing function throughout the company as a revenue generator as opposed to a cost center. We all know which functions get cut first. Cost centers get cut; revenue centers get funding.

Part IV - How to Do It

"The perfect is the enemy of the good." —Voltaire

B efore we delve into the how-to section, it is important that we set a level field by stating our assumptions. Prior to embarking on the new way strategy, your manufacturing firm must ensure that the operational side of the business is on par with the average. No matter how good and robust your marketing function is developed to be, a firm will not be able to gain market share if it is unable to produce, ship, and distribute a competitive product in a competitive way. Most manufacturing firms are up to speed on the operational side of the business. It is harder to gain an advantage with the production side of a manufacturing business because that has been the focus of most manufacturing firms over the past 100 years. Going forward, as we delineate how to gain a significant advantage with the new way strategy, we will assume your manufacturing firm is on par with average production, delivery, and distribution systems.

The second assumption is that you must apply this framework to one category at a time. If your firm is a smaller firm, one marketing plan and one go-to-market strategy will suit the entire company. If your firm is larger, with multiple business segments, you should choose one segment to begin with. It is a good idea to follow the profit/loss segment structure within your company. For example, if the P/L rolls up to a product category, each product category should be served by a separate go-to-market strategy. If the P/L rolls up to a business segment defined by a vertical industry, the go-to-market strategy should serve each business segment.

The third assumption is that you have either completed your marketing plan and will be revising the strategy and tactical portion according to the framework we are about to present, or, if you do not have an existing marketing plan, you are writing one in parallel with going through the new way framework.

Here we go.

Chapter 17 - The Audience Facing Mission Statement

Most companies think of a mission statement as the mission of the company. For example, we see a lot of mission statements that start off with "We offer high reliability and added value . . ." or "Our company mission is profitable growth through superior customer service, innovation, quality, and commitment" or "Our mission is to become the leading provider of blah, blah, blah." The one thing most of these mission statements have in common is that they are about what the company wants to be, do, or offer. They ignore the target audience. They try to match what they think their customers want to the mission statement. There may or may not be a place for this type of mission statement at your company; you will have to decide. Some firms think the company-facing mission statement helps to keep employees heading in the same direction. We will leave that discussion for another book.

The discussion going forward will be about a different type of mission statement, an audience-facing mission statement. We discussed the opportunity related to the sweet spot of engagement and the associated audience-facing mission statement (AFMS) back in Chapter 3. This section will be oriented toward crafting these two critical parts of the new way strategy.

Success will go to the company that is able to build its mission around the needs of the audience instead of around what the firm wants to be or thinks it wants to be. A manufacturing firm that makes its mission about solving a problem the people in the target audience face will win against competitors that continue to focus on using the mission statement to describe themselves. It is a somewhat subtle difference, but a significant difference.

In delineating the pains or passions of your target audience, it is important to fully understand those points of pain or passion. Many times, especially in more established companies, there is a type of collective or innate knowledge that gets passed around between the employees from generation to generation. This collective knowledge becomes a "known fact" after many years of everyone saying the same thing, but no one knows where this knowledge comes from. Before committing to the pain or passion point, I strongly recommended conducting some primary research with your target audience. In many cases, fresh primary research will refute the common knowledge shared by the employees. If your firm does not possess the competence to conduct a proper research study, outsource the project. Do not rely on a short informal survey of your customer base or prospective customer database. This type of informal survey will not give you an accurate analysis of the entire target audience.

Let me give you an example of the type of valuable information good primary research can unearth. As the global marketing director for a company that manufactured high-end measurement instruments, my marketing responsibility was within the life science industry. The common knowledge often touted by the sales and product teams was that our market share was above 40 percent and the brand was very well known among all life science companies. Some said that the brand was the market leader and every one of the big pharmaceutical companies knew the brand well.

I hired a firm to conduct primary market research, and the result completely refuted the collective knowledge. In fact, about 70 percent of the people in the life science target audience who had the responsibility of purchasing this specific type of measurement instrument had no idea of the name brand of their existing instrument. Even more telling was the fact that less than 5 percent of those polled had heard of our company brand. Wow! That revelation completely changed the way we decided to go to market.

To determine your audience-facing mission statement, you will draw on the target market information and decisions you determined in your marketing plan. Recall the sweet spot of engagement discussion in Part 1 and the sweet spot diagram, reprinted below.

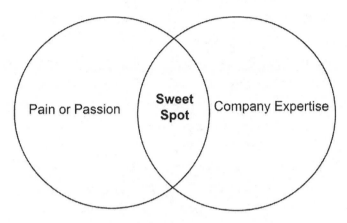

Sweet Spot of Engagement & AFMS

Follow these steps to determine your best audience-facing mission statement:

Step 1: Write down as many as five pain or passion points a majority of the people in your target audience (as defined in your marketing plan) exhibit. Each pain or passion point should be aligned with expertise that your company offers to help relieve the pain or fan the passion.

As an example of a pain point, if your manufacturing firm makes particle measurement instruments, some of the pain points might be (1) cannot rely on the measurement, (2) cannot get a repeatable measurement, (3) cannot keep the instrument within specifications.

If the firm manufactures industrial gloves to meet OSHA safety requirements, some target audience pain points might be (1) difficulty understanding OSHA regulations that apply to their plant, (2) difficulty knowing which type of glove to choose for various applications, (3) difficulty choosing a glove that fits correctly.

If your firm manufactures airplane navigation charts for general aviation pilots, some passion points might be (1) to be the best pilot in their respective community, (2) to get more enjoyment out of their hobby, (3) to create safe and secure flight plans.

Step 2: Write down the points of expertise that exist within your company. The expertise should not be about your products. Expertise and experts abound throughout your organization. Check out your R&D team, your customer service team, and your technical support team for experts with varying degrees of knowledge who can address the pain or passion points you chose in Step 1. When you approach the experts, be aware that they will be apprehensive about the time commitment or what will be required of them. They may be hesitant or even downright afraid you will ask them to write something or speak in front of a group. When you approach them about their expertise, be certain to reassure them that you, the marketer, will do all the work and all they will have to do is talk about their expertise. If you are lucky, you might find a few experts who want to write or speak, and that is a big added bonus!

For example, if your firm manufactures particle counters, you are not looking for an expert on how the instruments are made, you are looking for an expert who understands the different types of particle measuring technology and the pros and cons of each type.

As another example, if we go back to the company that manufactures humidity measurement instruments, they will likely have scientists on staff who know everything about the science of humidity and the associated measurement technologies. These experts would be a good source of information to help people relieve the pain of making poor and unreliable measurements.

Recalling the example of the firm that manufactures industrial gloves, a relevant expert would be one with knowledge about OSHA regulations and who has relationships with OSHA personnel.

Step 3: Describe the sweet spot of engagement, where the pain points and the expertise overlap. You should only choose one topic for the sweet spot. There are multiple lines included in the diagram so you can present multiple options for discussion. The sweet spot will be the intersection of one pain or passion point and one area of expertise. You may have identified more than one sweet spot for each, but you must select your best choice.

As an example, with the humidity instrument company, you might choose the pain point as being unable to rely on the instrument making a repeatable measurement. The expertise point might be knowledge of how the different types of technology work in various applications.

In the industrial glove company, the pain point might be a lack of understanding of OSHA regulations. The expertise point might be the knowledge held within the research and development team about relevant OSHA regulations.

In the particle measurement instrument company, the pain point might be not understanding the various ISO clean room standards and what must be done to comply. The expertise might be a thorough understanding about how to design and qualify a clean room for various applications.

Step 4: Craft the AFMS. Just to be clear, we are talking about engagement with people in the target audience at the top of the sales funnel. When the people make it to the bottom of the funnel, you will apply your product expertise, features, spec sheets, etc. You may even break out the product videos and product webinars at the bottom of the funnel, but for early audience engagement, which is where the money lies (revenue growth), you will need a guiding AFMS to drive your marketing decisions.

It is important to only focus on one topic at the intersection of pain and expertise. Do not discard your additional work (you can always use it later), but make sure you only work on one sweet spot at a time. The reason you should only choose one is because you will be developing content defined by the AFMS. It will be very important to evaluate your marketing activities to determine if your decision about the mission statement and the content was the correct choice. Developing more than one mission statement may be too much for your team. The prevailing assumption is that your manufacturing marketing team is limited in personnel, budget, and resources. If you happen to work in a company where marketing resources are abundant, it may be possible to develop more than one AFMS for multiple segments, product lines, etc. at the same time.

The audience-facing mission statement is very similar to a textbook positioning statement. There should be three parts to your mission statement:

1. **Target Market.** The target market should be defined based on criteria that can be segmented by such things as demographics, geography, psychographics, pains, needs, etc. "All" or "everyone" are not acceptable criteria.

2. **Pain or Passion.** Name the pain that your firm's expertise can relieve or name the passion that your firm's expertise can address.

3. **The Payoff.** This ties the pain or passion point with the needs or goals of the target audience. You need to tell the target audience how you will help them achieve what they want to achieve.

Your audience-facing mission statement might be constructed something like this:

"To help the people in our target audience of quality professionals in the pharmaceutical industry within the United States and Canada to make a more reliable, repeatable, and accurate measurement of humidity so that they can improve their production yield and prevent loss of product that may be caused by environmental variations."

"To help the people in our target audience of managers within the process industries to better understand and comply with OSHA regulations with respect to protective hand wear so they can keep their

employees safe and comply with government regulations, resulting in fewer workplace accidents and OSHA violations."

Now that you have your audience-facing mission statement, you are ready for the next step, a content audit and content creation plan.

Takeaway Actions:

1. Assemble your marketing team and go through the sweet spot exercise. The AFMS will be your guiding light. If a piece of content or an activity does not fit the AFMS, it should be rejected. If you are constructing your pilot program, the pilot activity must be aligned with the AFMS. It is also a helpful tool to use in explaining your rationale to management as to why you chose a certain pilot program.

Chapter 18 - Assess the Current Situation

This current situation is not the same as the current situation we spoke about in Chapter 7: The Marketing Plan. In this exercise, you are evaluating the current situation in the context of implementing your pilot program or your complete new way strategy. There are three areas of assessment you should undertake as you begin to execute your new way tactics:

- Content assessment
- Sales relationship assessment
- Product relationship assessment

Content Assessment

The purpose of the content assessment is to prepare the actual media for use in accordance with your audience-facing mission statement (AFMS). The first step is to evaluate the current state of your existing content. Determine if you have any existing content that conforms to the AFMS and is not a direct product promotion. You may have existing content that is close and could be very effective with a slight rework. For example, if you have an existing white paper that is in line with your AFMS but the last third of the paper promotes a product line, you could easily reformat the paper to be useful and helpful without touting the product. It takes much less time, energy, and money to repurpose content as compared to creating brand-new content. Always keep in mind that if a piece of content (whether existing, repurposed, or proposed) does not support the AFMS, it should not be used. Types of content may include a mixture of any of these items:

- Papers
- Technical notes
- Application notes
- EBooks

- Infographics
- Webinars
- Seminars
- Frequently asked questions
- Videos
- Podcasts
- How-to guides
- And more . . .

Creating content can be a fun and exhilarating project. It's easy to get caught up in the creation process, but when creating content, keep in mind that you are always better off creating fewer higher-quality pieces of content rather than going crazy and creating a high volume of mediocre content that loses touch with the AFMS.

I recommend creating a big poster emblazoned with your AFMS and posting it in your marketing area. Do not lose sight of the mission statement. Many companies will start with the creation of content with quantity being the driving goal. This is a big mistake and must be avoided at all costs. Each and every piece of content must be high quality, useful, and support the mission statement.

Again, to clarify, the AFMS is designed for audience engagement at the top of the funnel, in the "get to know us" stage of building an eventual customer relationship. Content that is about the product and its features and benefits is in a separate category, not to be discussed here. Most manufacturing companies are very good at the product content but very weak in the engagement phase content. We are focusing on the top of the funnel in this section.

Before you start to create a lot of new content, which can be expensive and resource intensive, conduct a content audit. There is a high likelihood of there being some useable content within your organization's archives, content that supports your mission statement. The archived content will probably need an update and a makeover, but it may very well be useful. I worked for a company that manufactured aviation navigation charts. During the content audit, I found a treasure trove of articles that were more than ten years old. I asked around about the articles (which were included in old-fashioned printed newsletters) and to my delight, some of the old-timers said those articles were a huge hit back in the old days of ten years ago. We were able to repurpose them as blog posts with a little updating of the data and, sure enough, they were a huge hit again ten years later. It probably took 10 percent of the money and resources to repurpose the old content as compared to creating new content from scratch. Repurposing content can be a gold mine for your marketing team.

One last point on content creation: It is a good idea to get a sense of the type of media the people in your target audience will consume. In an April 2014 research study by TREW Marketing, it was revealed that the number one choice of content for engineers was to download a PDF file. If your audience likes to download files and print out the content, you would be wise to provide them with the most relevant format. It would not be wise to provide this audience with an infographic or a video if they are not consuming that type of content. Find some third-party research about how your particular audience consumes content as you make your decisions about content types.

Sales Relationship Assessment

Another area to evaluate as you assess your organization's readiness for the new way is the status of the relationship between the marketing and sales teams and the associated leadership. You can be successful with this type of marketing strategy without the support of the sales team. It may be the case that the sales folks only care about getting leads and they don't care how marketing finds the leads. If that is the case, I encourage you to proceed with a pilot program in accordance with Part 3 but without the involvement of sales. I guarantee that as soon as you start to have success, sales will eventually come around and jump on the bandwagon. However, if your organization does have a healthy, collaborative relationship between marketing and sales, you will see better results and you will see those results faster with an aligned revenue team.

Do the sales and marketing leadership collaborate or do they work in separate silos? If the culture is such that they work in separate silos, it might be difficult to get the sales team involved. Is there animosity between the marketing and sales functions? This is not uncommon in manufacturing organizations. If there is animosity, your task will be much harder, but do not give up easily. I suggest you pursue your pilot program in spite of the animosity. Is marketing perceived as the toady to sales? If yes, it will take sales longer to realize your newfound budding role of revenue generator, but it will happen eventually.

Product Team Relationship Assessment

In many manufacturing companies, the product group runs the show and wields heavy influence. As a marketer, you may even report to the product manager. Some members of the marketing organization may have the title product marketing manager. If your hierarchy is such that your leadership is embedded in the product group, your challenge will be difficult. Imagine the looks you will get when you tell your boss, the product marketing manager, that you recommend top-of-the-funnel activities should cease and desist talking about the product features. Do not despair. Go back to Part 3 and proceed with a pilot program. Even the most ardent product culture perceives itself as creative and innovative. It would be hard for the product manager to deny your initiative in demonstrating innovation and creativity without appearing hypocritical.

Upon completion of your three-part assessment, you should have a good understanding of what you are up against as far as the existing content, sales team alignment, and product culture. At this point you should have the following assets in place:

- A few pieces of educational content in a few different formats

- A subject matter expert or two ready, willing, and able to provide expertise in line with your audience-facing mission statement
- An understanding of your organization and the level of difficulty you will face with the culture change
- A plan to overcome the identified hurdles with a comprehensive new way pilot program

Takeaway Actions:

1. Conduct a three-part assessment as outlined above.
2. Build a network of supporters based on what you learn about the politics of your existing structure.

Chapter 19 - Best Chance Tactics for Success

Assuming your manufacturing organization is like the firms we have been discussing, with a strong product culture and a low-influence marketing department, you might only have one shot at proving the worth of the new way strategy. If you have followed my advice so far and have laid the groundwork for a pilot program, it is likely that you were given support to proceed. There are a few tactics that will give you a much higher chance of success.

A best chance tactic has three specific criteria. First, the tactic must easily demonstrate meaningful numbers that show engagement. Because the ability to show numbers is important, that means the tactic must have a call to action that can be counted. Second, the data you count must include the contact information. In other words, the count should not be anonymous, such as clicks or likes. Third, the topic must resonate with and be highly relevant to the people in your target audience as defined by your audience-facing mission statement.

One example of a tactic that fits these criteria is an educational webinar series. Webinars are perfect for producing meaningful numbers. A webinar allows you to collect meaningful numbers such as registrants and attendees to the live broadcast. A webinar also requires registrants to provide their contact information. The reason webinars are so conducive to counting and capturing contact information is the built-in call to action of the registration form. One could argue that the list of attendees is a list of qualified leads. Qualified leads are a very strong success metric. Imagine being able to tell your stakeholders that your pilot program webinar garnered 253 qualified leads. This type of result will all but guarantee a continuation of your pilot program and an affirmation of the new way strategy.

The critically important component that will ensure success of the webinar is a relevant topic. If your topic is in line with the AFMS, you will get good numbers. If you demur in the face of criticism or pressure from the sales or product stakeholders and allow the topic to be about a product, you will lose and your pilot program may be all for naught. You are better off not doing anything than doing a webinar about the product if your goal is to engage the greater target audience (which it should be). See Appendix 1 for a complete eight-step framework for creating a lead-generating webinar pilot or series.

Another example of a tactic that has a high chance of success is the opt-in educational enewsletter. An opt-in enewsletter is delivered via email on a consistent and regular schedule. The opt-in definition means you do not blast it to everyone in your database. By only sending the enewsletter to those who request it, you must prove the value of the content in the email or you lose your subscribers. An opt-in enewsletter will perform about three times better than a blast enewsletter as measured by open and click-through rates.

In many instances, when a manufacturing marketer thinks about a newsletter of any kind, they conjure up a two- or three-page document with news stories that are solicited from the various operational groups in the company. Articles about a new employee, new product, community service, and some company news typically populate this newsletter. That is the wrong way. Do not, under any circumstances, use an enewsletter for your pilot program if the content will be about the company, its employees, or the products. It will fail. The best chance enewsletter will contain one story and one article as defined by the AFMS. It is okay to include an ad strip with some company news, but the ad strip should not dominate the enewsletter. Sometimes you have to include a product promotion in the ad strip to appease the product and sales team leaders.

The format that works best to gain and keep subscribers is one with a theme defined by the AFMS. The enewsletter should promote a high-value content asset, but not completely contain the asset. An abstract with a thumbnail picture is enough. The reader of the enewsletter clicks on the asset link to download the full piece of content. This type of enewsletter does two very valuable things: it gives control to the subscriber and it supports the AFMS by providing information, education, or knowledge about a pain point that is common to the target audience. The opt-in enewsletter allows for a count and captures contact information, since people must provide, at the very least, an email address. See Appendix 2 for a detailed execution plan to create an opt-in enewsletter.

In the example we discussed earlier, a company that manufactures measurement instruments for humidity defined the AFMS as "To help the people in our target audience make a more reliable, repeatable, and accurate measurement of humidity." A good theme for an enewsletter supporting this company's AFMS could be "Humidity Theory, Terms, and Definitions." Each enewsletter would include a synopsis of an article and an option to click through to read the whole article about humidity parameter definitions, for example.

Because your call to action is for someone to subscribe, you get a natural count of engagement and it is fairly easy to compare the subscribers' purchasing behaviors to the purchasing behavior of your entire database. Assuming the subscribers purchase more and more often as compared to the general database, you will have another strong metric supporting the success of your enewsletter pilot program.

I have seen many manufacturing companies start out with a blog as their pilot program. Starting with a blog by itself is a mistake. It's hard to get a good count of people reading your blog, and it's difficult to capture the contact information of the people reading your blog. A blog will not show up in organic search results unless it is tightly optimized. Even with a blog that is optimized for search, it takes a considerable length of time before it starts to show up in search results and generating web traffic. If you are not able to optimize each and every post, your blog will not be found. According to the website statista.com, there were 260.5 million blogs on the Internet as of October 2015. So there are a lot of blogs out there, and it takes a long time for them to get any traction. The other danger of starting with a blog is that it is hard for most manufacturing companies to sustain a regular cadence. Some statistics state that as many as 95 percent of all blogs have been abandoned.

While a blog by itself is a poor tactic for your pilot program, the combination of an opt-in enewsletter and a blog is a powerful tactic. You gain the meaningful numbers and contact information from the email subscription. The enewsletter content is easily repurposed for the blog and the content on the blog page is good for organic search results.

Takeaway Actions:

1. Choose a pilot program tactic that contains the three critical components: meaningful numbers that show engagement, identification of the contacts, and a highly relevant topic.
2. Webinars and enewsletters are the two tactics that work best. If you have the resources available, couple your opt-in enewsletter with a blog, but do not use a blog by itself as your pilot program tactic.

Chapter 20 - 'New Way' Tools and Technology

At this point, you have chosen your best chance tactic for your pilot program, created the content, and you are ready to execute. Your goal is to engage with your target audience in a meaningful way by helping them be better, thereby creating TOMA, credibility, and reciprocity. When the day comes around and the people in your target audience (who have benefited from your helpful content) are ready to buy the type of product you manufacture, you are very likely to get the business over your laggard competitor who is still pitching product features and benefits.

As discussed in Chapter 12, there are some essential tools you will need in order to execute the pilot program and measure and report on the results. If your pilot program is a success and you gain support in expanding the new way to go to market, the tool set becomes even more essential for scaling your new marketing strategy. You will need tools for the following components of your pilot program and, ultimately, your new way marketing strategy.

Database: If you have not already installed a customer relationship management (CRM) tool, now is the time to get that tool in place. If the state of your contact database is such that customers are in one system, marketing prospects are in spreadsheet files, and the sales team keeps their prospective customers in a secret spreadsheet only accessible to them, you have a big problem. If you are not able to aggregate all customer, prospective customer, and marketing contacts into one database such as a CRM, you will have a very, very difficult time demonstrating success with your pilot program. You could pull off a successful webinar without a CRM, but the effort could prove futile if you are not able to provide a robust follow-up process. Without a CRM and an email service provider (ESP), it is next to impossible to manage an effective enewsletter program. Should you proceed without a database tool? Yes, but it will be five to ten times more difficult. If you are in this boat, your best bet will be to get some outside help from a marketing professional who is an expert in email and/or webinar production. Refer to Chapter 12 for more information about the CRM tool. A quick fix to this problem is to use your email service provider database tool.

Distribution: At the risk of stating the obvious, you will need a tool that allows you to communicate digitally with the people in your target audience about your content. The people in your target audience cannot realize the value if your educational content or engage with it and your manufacturing firm's brand unless they are informed.

For an email enewsletter, you will need an email service provider. A few of the more common providers were listed in Chapter 12. The requirements for an email service provider include the ability to create an HTML email, maintain an email database, send the email to a selected list, and measure the results. Results include the open rate, click-to-open rate, click-through rate, unsubscribe rate, and opt-in rate. If you choose to couple a blog with your enewsletter, you will need a tool to host and manage the blog posts. The blog tool should enable measurement of the engagement via downloads and/or views.

If you choose the webinar as your content choice, you will need a webinar platform or a marketing automation platform. Most webinar platforms include all the tools you need for webinar distribution. In this case, I mean distribution as in the entire stream of interactions from the email invitation to the final post-webinar measurement. A marketing automation platform working in conjunction with a webinar platform allows a more flexible distribution stream and more refined metrics. By more flexible, I mean you can customize the emails, landing page, and hyperlinks for better measurement and for better engagement as determined by registrations and attendance.

Measurement: As mentioned, some of the distribution tools will have built-in measurement tools. Marketing automation and most CRMs include robust measurement tools. As you launch your pilot program, measurement of the key performance indicators will be critical to prove the effectiveness of the new way strategy. Whatever tools you choose, you must be able to offer comprehensive measurement of the results so you can discuss and present the numbers, as mentioned above and in Chapter 19, for best chance tactics.

There are many tools and combinations to choose from in this modern digital age. Some of the features may overlap, and that is acceptable. What is not acceptable is a tool set that is missing any of the components I've listed.

Now you are ready to go ahead and execute your pilot program. You may have doubts about your choices and certainly, if your culture is a strong product culture, there may be a lot on the line. My advice is to forge ahead and execute. Just do it, as some would say. If you follow the recommendations and steps presented here, you will see success and you will be poised for even greater success with your new way to go to market strategy.

Takeaway Actions:

1. Review Chapter 12 and choose your supporting technology, ensuring you will have the capability to manage your database, distribute content, and measure the results.

2. At a minimum, you must have an email service provider, webinar platform, and blog-hosting platform, depending on the particular pilot program tactic you choose. A marketing automation platform is ideal, but be aware of the potential pitfalls of this technology. See Appendix 3 for more information about the pros and cons of marketing automation.

Chapter 21 - What about Social Media?

Ah yes, social media. How could social media not be included as a part of the new way strategy? Social media is not a strategy, and it is not a tactic. Social media is merely a channel, and it may or may not be an appropriate channel for your audience. As an example, many manufacturing companies feel compelled to put up a Facebook page without ever considering if their audience is active on Facebook and wants to engage in the content you offer there. As an example, suppose my company manufactures fancy widgets. My target audience is engineers who work at semiconductor manufacturing companies. It may be true that engineers who work at semiconductor companies are present on Facebook, but they likely are not on Facebook to advance their careers or to solve issues they face on the job. They are probably there to see what friends and relatives are doing in their lives and to share their own lives with pictures, stories, etc. If this is the case, does it make sense for the fancy widget company to put in any time and energy into Facebook? I would counsel restraint if your situation is similar. The caveat is, as with any marketing channel, that you should feel free to test it and see if your hypothesis is correct. Your preconception may be right or it may be wrong.

As a side note, Facebook has changed its algorithm significantly in the last year and continues to update the algorithm on a regular basis. With these changes, it has become clear that if you want your commercial message to show up in the feed or on the page, you have to pay. There is virtually no such thing as free organic reach on Facebook for any type of commercial message.

The same consideration should be made for any social media channel: Pinterest, Instagram, Twitter, LinkedIn, Disqus, Snapchat, SlideShare, et al. Ask and answer the question "Is my target audience present on this social media channel for the purpose of consuming the content I provide?" If the answer is yes, the channel may be viable to support your audience-engagement goals. If the answer is no, then you should not use the channel. Further, if you do answer yes, then determine if the channel will support your goals and your AFMS.

Suppose you can answer yes for multiple social media channels, should you be on every channel that is a fit? It is tempting, but I suggest limiting activity in social media to fewer channels as compared to more channels. It has been proven that regular, frequent, and relevant posting is more effective than sporadic posting. Naturally, it will depend on your marketing team resource pool, but few channels with more robust distribution of content are preferred over more channels with thin streams of content. As with any channel, be sure to measure engagement and, if possible, measure influence on pipeline and revenue to determine if you are getting a return on your marketing investment.

Should you choose to use certain social media channels as a tactic, be certain the posts are in line with the audience-facing mission statement. Each and every channel and activity must support the AFMS. Social media is especially susceptible to drifting away from the AFMS. It is easy to post on social channels and especially easy to fall into the pattern of pitching products. The same rule applies to social channels as to all channels as you adopt the new way strategy: STOP PITCHING PRODUCTS! Social media is good for engaging at the top of the funnel, assuming your audience is present as described above. If there is one thing you should have learned by now, pitching products does not work for top-of-the-funnel engagement, regardless of the channel.

Takeaway Actions:

1. Audit your current social media activity. Determine which channels are active. Assess the level of activity on each social media channel and determine exactly who is posting and what they are posting. Is there a coherent strategy or mission behind the social media activity?

2. If your firm is active on social media channels, is there a reason for posting that supports the business objectives? Has the reason been

written down and agreed to by the stakeholders? If there is no reason, goal, or mission supporting the social media activity, consider putting resources elsewhere or create social media guidelines for company posting.

Chapter 22 - After the Pilot Program

Your pilot program was a success! You chose a relevant and engaging topic. You chose a tactic that resulted in concrete numbers and contact information. You delivered qualified leads to the top of the sales funnel. You superstars even used an integrated MAP and CRM to demonstrate a strong influence on closed/won opportunities, a.k.a. revenue. You have been given the go-ahead and the resources to expand your fledgling innovative and creative new way strategy. So what's next?

If your pilot was exceptionally successful, you will have garnered attention from the highest levels of the organization. This can be good and it can be bad. It is good if the attention results in additional resources such as money and people as well as support for your innovation and creativity. Another positive outcome of high-level attention could be momentum in moving against the strong product-based culture we discussed in Part 3. If the CEO recognizes the concept of marketing without pitching the product for top-of-the-funnel engagement, you can bet the product managers will also pay attention to the new way strategy.

Depending on your company culture, high-level attention as a result of your success could also arouse negative feelings of contempt and jealousy among some of the leadership team or some of the higher-level managers. This is especially dangerous if the resources you are given come out of the resources of another department such as product development or sales. There are some people who just do not like to see others succeed. Depending on the influencers and their feelings toward the success of the marketing function, your pilot program and your plan to move forward could be in a precarious situation. If you find yourself in this type of situation, it is important to collaborate and find a high-level champion, preferably someone on the leadership team, who will support your fledgling marketing strategy.

Another pitfall you may encounter because of your success is in colleagues asking (or demanding) that you develop content and programs not aligned with the audience-facing mission statement. Stay true to your mission statement and do not give in to any requests or demands to start pitching products. If your collaboration effort was strong when you were building the foundation of your pilot program and the associated mission statement, you will have the wherewithal to say no to these requests. Hint: When you are building out your pilot program and the mission statement, incorporate it to your overarching marketing plan and get sign-off from the stakeholders.

Depending on the resources you have been given, after a successful pilot program it is time to further your engagement tactics as defined by the AFMS by creating additional content or repurposing existing content. It is also wise to include additional channels or increase distribution in your success channel. If you chose educational webinars as your pilot tactic, expand on the webinar series with additional webinars and by repurposing the webinar content into other formats. You should post webinar recordings on your website and on YouTube or other video-hosting sites. Craft FAQs and infographics from the webinar content. If you have uncovered a couple of subject matter experts who are enthusiastic about your new way pilot program, craft a new webinar series in line with the AFMS.

If your pilot program was the combination of an enewsletter and a blog, start additional enewsletters and build out a subscription center. There is really no limit to the number of enewsletters and associated blogs you can launch (subject to your level of resources, of course).

What if your pilot program was not successful? Although this type of engagement marketing has been proven to work in most manufacturing companies, there is a chance that your pilot program might not live up to expectations. If your first pilot did not meet expectations, you have a few options:

1. Give up on the idea and return to the mundane tasks of setting up trade shows, creating product brochures, and doing whatever the sales and product teams tell you to do. I

say this tongue in cheek. I really do not want you to give up on the new way strategy, just keep on working at it and you will eventually see success.

2. Try again, with a different sweet spot and AFMS.

3. Get outside help from a marketing consultant who specializes in working with manufacturing companies and has a proven track record of success.

The bottom line is the same as with any marketing strategy, tactic, or activity: do more of what works and stop doing what is not working. The term works is subjective and should be defined by the chosen key performance indicators you have agreed upon. A great reference book for building out a content marketing strategy is Epic Content Marketing by Joe Pulizzi. This book outlines how to expand on a successful pilot program and ultimately completely change the way your manufacturing firm executes its marketing strategy.

Takeaway Actions:

1. Make sure you have a clear plan with clear metrics to determine your pilot program's level of success. Be honest and transparent about the success or lack thereof that you experience with your pilot. Share the results with your stakeholders.

2. If your pilot program was a success, do not be afraid to ask for more resources and support to expand on the new way concept. Do more of what works and stop doing what is not working.

3. If your pilot was not a success, don't give up. Review your plan to determine what went wrong. Was it too much about a product and not enough about a topic the audience cares about? Did you misread the pain point of the target audience? Did your experts fail to convey real authority on the subject? Identify the problem and try again. This type of marketing strategy has been proven to work and it will work for you too.

Part V - One Revenue Team

"Insanity: doing the same thing over and over again, but expecting different results." —*Albert Einstein*

Chapter 23 - Seat at the Leadership Table

T he marketing leader rarely occupies a seat at the leadership table of a manufacturing company. Most manufacturing companies' leadership team or executive team typically includes the chief executive officer, chief finance officer, chief human resources officer, chief operations officer, and a representative of the business segment, either sales or product. Why is marketing conspicuously absent? The reason is twofold. The executive team does not understand marketing, and the executive team does not respect marketing.

Granted, this is probably not true in every manufacturing organization. B2C manufacturing is likely to respect their marketing team a bit more than their B2B counterparts. Based on my experience and anecdotal evidence, I feel confident in saying the vast majority of B2B manufacturing companies do not respect their marketing team or marketing as a discipline. To verify this statement, all you need to do is look at the marketing activities and advertisements put out by manufacturing companies. They are usually terrible, and you cannot blame the marketers. The marketers want to be better and want to do better, but the powers within the manufacturing organization (sales, product, or executive) do not support marketing with resources and, even worse, force very poor ideas on the marketing professionals. Advertisements appear to be either done in-house by someone who has no idea about design or layout fundamentals or they are done by an advertising agency. Marketing is getting no respect in either case.

Marketing is divided into two areas: strategy and tactics. Strategic marketing is usually formulated (and I use this term loosely) by the big boys and girls at the leadership table. The marketing leader does not belong to this self-proclaimed elite group. We have a group of executives who know nothing about practical marketing strategy or marketing tactics making decisions that are usually based on the latest sales or product person's shallow insight or the latest product under development. They will try to bring their own personal experiences of being "marketed to" into the discussion. This leadership team will likely include the CEO, CFO, CHRO, and business segment leaders, none of whom will have had any practical marketing experience. Strategic marketing will usually be reduced to a few catchphrases, for example, "We have to be more customer focused" or "We have to use more digital marketing."

It is from these types of meetings that strategic decisions about social media are born. It sounds something like this: The CEO says, "Hey, my daughter spends all of her time on Facebook. Did you know there are more than a billion users of Facebook?" Then the head of HR pipes up and says, "Yeah, my son is on Twitter and he loves it. He's majoring in marketing at State U this year. He says social media really boosts a company's SEO, too." The CFO says, "What's SEO?" They all have a good laugh and assign someone to tell Rita the marketing manager to get the company up on Facebook and Twitter as they move on to the quarterly income statement. Sadly, but alas typically, that type of conversation serves as the marketing strategy discussion with the leadership team.

In the meantime, the servant class of marketer takes care of the tactical marketing, which includes the daily activities called "marketing," such as trade shows, advertisements, email blasts, etc. These disrespected marketing team members spend their time and energy reacting to the sales team or the product team. In many cases, product marketing leads the marketing team. Even worse, in many manufacturing companies, the engineering team leads marketing. Ask any manufacturing marketer about what engineers think of marketing, and you will see the marketer's eyes roll around and his or her head shake back and forth.

Recall the VP of engineering/marketing I mentioned in Chapter 11, when he revealed his idea about what was needed from marketing. He wanted to see "pizzazz" and "flamboyance" from the marketing team. He was completely clueless about marketing strategy, tactics, or what a marketing team should be doing for a manufacturing organization, yet he held a seat at the leadership table and contributed to the marketing strategy in a format similar to the social media discussion I mention above. This particular VP was also very excited about the coming year, which would be the company's fiftieth anniversary. He expected the poor marketers to expend a lot of time, energy, and budget toward the promotion, and meanwhile sales were lagging behind the previous year. I told him that nobody in his target audience cared about how many years the company had been in business. I told him they cared about WIIFM. He gave me a blank stare, and I was never invited back to that company.

Marketing can and should be a powerful revenue-generating force within all manufacturing companies. In this day and age, marketing should be leading the entire revenue team, including sales, marketing, inside sales, and product management. A modern, smart, adept marketing leader and organization has much to offer. Why is it that there is little mention of marketing in most manufacturing professional organizations? There is plenty of discussion around "lean manufacturing," "supply chain management," "Six Sigma," etc., but very little mention of marketing. Oh, but there is one discussion where marketing is talked about and brought into the conversation, and that is when budgets must be cut. When budget cuts need to be made, invariably someone on the leadership team will say, "We can always cut our marketing spend."

Although it is true that most B2B manufacturing organizations have very little respect for marketing, the upside is the huge opportunity for the manufacturing business and its executives who are willing to change this no-respect-for-marketing culture. Smart marketing leaders are in a perfect position to promote marketing as a source of revenue and a driver of business strategy. Marketing leaders and the professionals who make up their teams are ready, willing, and able to step up to the demand for growth. Professional marketers know how to drive engagement, fill the top of the funnel, create TOMA, and, most important, grow the business. Most manufacturing leaders embrace innovation and creativity as a cornerstone of their business. There is no more innovative and creative group of people than the modern marketing team. There is not a more exciting opportunity to innovate than embracing, respecting, and creating a revenue-driving marketing team. Yes, I am a professional marketer and I am proud of my profession. As marketers, we have the technology, tools, and the knowledge to contribute at the leadership table. We, the professional marketers, are ready to earn the respect of the manufacturing organization if given the opportunity.

It should be every marketing leader's driving ambition to claim his or her seat at the leadership table. The way to make this happen is to talk the talk of the C-suite and prove contribution to the business goals as discussed in Chapter 16. We can and we must advance the practice of marketing within the manufacturing industry. It is time for all of us manufacturing marketers to work together toward a goal of positioning the marketing function as the leader of the revenue-creation group.

Takeaway Actions:

1. Decide if you want and/or deserve a seat at the executive leadership table. Identify what perceptions would have to change to make it happen. Do you believe you, as the marketing leader, have the knowledge and experience to contribute to the business strategy and run the revenue team?

2. Determine if there is a marketing strategy void in your leadership team. Assess the current leadership team's decisions and make a determination of whether the marketing strategy is sound or if it is made by seat-of-the-pants discussions as described in this chapter.

3. If you are the marketing leader and you answer yes to the actions listed above, make a plan to claim your seat at the table.

Accoording to SiriusDecisions, companies that have achieved sales and marketing alignment see an average annual increase in revenue of 24 percent, close 500 percent more leads, and are more than 600 percent more profitable.

Alignment is difficult and uncommon in the manufacturing sector. Ask these questions to determine if your firm has aligned sales and marketing: Does the sales team know what the marketing team is doing on a daily basis and on a strategic basis to influence revenue? Does sales know the positioning statement, value proposition, target market, and associated messaging? Does the marketing team know which daily activities the sales team is performing? Does the marketing team understand the salespeople's needs, wants, frustrations, likes, or dislikes about marketing activities or content? In many cases, the answer to these questions is a resounding no on both sides. There is much writing and commiserating about the topic of sales and marketing alignment. Alignment between these seemingly disparate functions is very hard to achieve. However, data shows that the firm that is able to accomplish alignment will significantly outperform those firms that do not achieve alignment.

As a former manager of a global marketing team responsible for regional execution of marketing activities, I experienced the difficulty of achieving alignment nearly every day. Sales is busy and focused on doing everything they can to sell more product because their income depends on meeting quota. Marketing is working hard to generate demand through events, brochures, emails, etc. And never the twain shall meet, as they say. My experience tells me that the critical piece of the alignment puzzle is direction from the top of the chain of command. Without a leader focusing on alignment it will never happen. Ideally, I suggest a structure with one senior person leading both teams. A strong leader would ensure that all of the questions posed above would be answered with a resounding yes. The ubiquitous structure found throughout the manufacturing industry, consisting of a separate sales team and a separate marketing team with different leaders, should be abolished and replaced with the single revenue team under one leader. Once this structure is changed, you are in a much better position to achieve alignment within one team versus struggling to align what commonly is seen as two empires.

Marketing and sales alignment is not enough. As long as the organization continues to perceive two different functions or units with very different goals and perceptions, the company will be at odds with itself. It is time to abolish the terms, perception, and structure of these two teams. It is time to unite sales and marketing under one leader, one mission, one culture, and one set of goals. Meet the One Revenue Team.

Takeaway Action:

1. Evaluate your current company structure around the revenue-generating side of the business. Answer each of the questions posed in this chapter.

Chapter 25 - One Revenue Team

he revenue team is responsible for generating and delivering revenue. Some would call this team the commercial team, but I prefer to include the word revenue, as it emphasizes the overarching purpose of this team. The mission of the revenue team is to find customers, engage them, build relationships, develop trust, close business, and cultivate ongoing customer relationships; in other words, everything to do with acquiring new customers, taking care of existing customers, and maintaining customer relationships.

The revenue team must be headed by a person with both marketing and sales experience. If the leader lacks expertise in either of these disciplines, he will tend to favor his own proficiency and is likely to cultivate the team in a lopsided manner. In addition to sales and marketing experience, the leader must understand business finance and be able to speak with the executive team using C-suite language, the language of finance. The leader should have an advanced degree in business and must possess consummate knowledge of the latest marketing strategy, tactics, and technology as well as the sales channel strategy, tactics, and technology.

The revenue team will be comprised of people who once worked in departments called field sales, marketing, inside sales, key account management, customer support, order processing, application engineering, telemarketing, corporate communications, etc. You get the idea. These departments and associated titles or labels should be abolished when the manufacturing firm makes the evolution to a "one revenue team" model. The associated job descriptions will remain fairly consistent with the old model, with the main exception being those who once worked in the marketing department. Marketing will take an active role in generating revenue and not a backseat to the sales team, as they most likely have grown accustomed to over the years.

By uniting all of the functions listed above into one revenue team, the sales and marketing alignment issue is resolved. The entire revenue team will be striving toward a unified objective and associated goals under one leader. This is the power of one revenue team. Another benefit of uniting these disparate functions under one leader and one team is that it does away with the bickering and the battles for resources between the function leaders. With each and every member of revenue on board and going in the same direction, amazing success will be the result.

The transformation from separate sales and marketing teams with separate leadership will usually be a very big cultural change in most manufacturing companies. The change may or may not result in termination of some key positions within the organization, or it may result in adding positions. Big organizational changes are difficult and require strong change management skills to be exercised by all leaders in the organization, especially the revenue team leader. You will be changing some employees' core self-image (I'm talking about the field sales team mostly). In many manufacturing organizations, sales is used to calling the shots and enjoys strong influence with the executive team. Without the support of the CEO, a change this big will be extremely difficult if not impossible. Get the CEO on board as the main change agent.

If you decide to make the change and use the one revenue team model, collaboration and communication are essential. Do not keep it a secret and then spring it on the affected employees on the first day of the year or quarter. Keep everyone in the loop, explain the benefits, and be honest about the differences and difficulty of making the switch. Not everyone will be on board. The field sales team will be wary of how it will affect their compensation and their freedom. The marketing team will be wary about their newly established responsibility for revenue. Approach this conversion as you would any large organizational change, in accordance with best practices, and you will see the benefits.

How do you know if your new one revenue team organization is working? It's easy: just look at the financial results of revenue growth and profitability. If the growth rate is increasing and better than it was prior to the change, it's working. A stronger indicator is if profit grows along with revenue. I recommend using the net-contribution metric discussed in Chapter 7. Naturally, it is important to track other key performance indicators for each of the various activities under the revenue team. Depending the compensation model your firm uses, a powerful driver of success would be to put the entire team under one bonus structure.

Takeaway Actions:

1. Consider the "one revenue team" model in the context of your organization. If your sales and marketing teams are not aligned, this model may be just the thing to springboard your business goals. Craft a plan to enable one revenue team. Put it in writing. Practice your pitch.

2. Seek out examples of manufacturing companies using this type of model and ask them about it. If they are not direct competitors, they will likely share the pitfalls and successes of their journey.

T he time has come for the manufacturing marketer to take his or her rightful place at the leadership table. Manufacturing companies can no longer afford to ignore the contribution of the modern marketer. Each and every manufacturing company must leverage the new marketing strategy, tactics, and tools if the firm is to survive global competition and the relatively new ease of purchasing enabled by the World Wide Web.

Those manufacturing companies that ignore the new reality of how their customers and prospective customers go through the buying process, without the aid of a salesperson until the very end of the process, will lose market share to those who are willing and able to embrace the new way strategy. This is not your grandfather's or even your father's marketplace, where customer development relied on personal relationships from the very start of engagement. The old-school sales model of feet on the street is no longer effective for growing a manufacturing business. At best, that model will maintain the existing business. At worst, it will cause firms to lose market share rapidly to the manufacturing firms that read this book and embrace the new way. Tradeshows, postcards, print ads, field sales teams, and even distributors will not be able to compete without leveraging the new normal, where prospective customers self-educate, research, and build relationships with firms before they ever send an email or pick up the phone. It's happening, baby. The train is leaving the station. The window is closing.

Engaging with the people in your target audience takes more, much more, than telling them about your products and your company. If you do not understand the audience's pain and problems beyond the relationship to your product features, you will lose. Those manufacturing companies that engage with their audience by helping them to be better by sharing expertise will destroy the firms that continue to rely on old-style sales and marketing tactics alone.

There is a massive opportunity for those firms that can embrace the new way to go to market. Most manufacturing firms will ignore this advice. Others will be unable or unwilling to change the way they go to market. Most of the executives who read or hear about this book will discount the idea because their product leaders and their sales leaders will tell them it will not work. These sales and product leaders speak out of self-preservation and fear, but the new way should not be perceived as a threat. The sales and product teams are still important if not essential components of the firm, and they need to allow marketing to step up and share the responsibility.

If you are satisfied with annual growth rates of 3 to 5 percent this year and 2 to 3 percent next year and 0 to 1 percent the following year, then you should continue what you have been doing in the marketing arena for the past fifty years. If you want to grow your business organically by 10 percent, 20 percent, or 30 percent, the only way left, the last frontier, is to leverage the new way and embrace the marketing function as a strategic component of the business.

If you do not believe your current marketing leader and her team are capable of stepping up and making these crucial changes, hire a new marketing leader and a new team, if necessary. If your existing leader does not understand the concepts we have been presenting in this book, get one who does understand them, but be quick because first movers will win.

Write a marketing plan if you do not already have one. Discover the sweet spot for audience engagement at the intersection of the audience pain point and your firm's expertise. Engage with the greater audience by helping them to be better. Get TOMA, credibility, and reciprocity to gain more customers and increase growth rates. Use modern tools such as a marketing automation platform integrated with a CRM. Include your head marketer in the strategy discussions and listen to what he has to say. Finally, create a "one revenue team" model and abolish the old silos of sales and marketing.

The new way to go to market will eventually catch on, just like everything else in business that is proven to work. You have to be first or second in your competitive market space to gain market share. When your competition starts to see their market share shrink and their annual growth rates slow to 0 percent and they notice your growth accelerating and your market share increasing, get ready for them to jump on board with their own new way strategy. The window is closing, and the first movers will win.

Takeaway Actions:

1. Get started right away. Do not wait. While you wait to better understand the strategy or wait for your growth rate to stall completely, your competition is executing. Be the first mover.

2. If you are not the marketing leader or an executive leader at your manufacturing firm, try to get them to read this book. Propose a pilot program. Prove the effectiveness of the new way with an A/B test pitting product promotion against knowledge promotion.

Step 1: Get together with your key stakeholders to agree on these foundational concepts:

- Define the objective for the webinar. It could be leads, closed business, awareness, or something else supporting the business goals.
- Identify the target audience and where they can be reached.
- Select the topic for the webinar. The first ideas you hear will be to promote your wonderful product. RESIST! Product-based webinars will fail. The webinar topic should be of an educational nature. Educate the target audience about something that matters to them. Your firm should have unique expertise on this topic. See Chapters 3 and 17 for more information about choosing a topic with the sweet spot of engagement and the audience-facing mission statement.
- Agree on the metrics you will use to determine success or failure: number of registrants, attendees, or fulfillment of some other call to action.
- Agree with the sales team on their role in promoting and/or following up on the webinar.
- Gain agreement on budget and personnel resources. Personnel resources are especially important if your subject matter experts will be contributing their expertise and knowledge on top of their regular duties and responsibilities.

Step 2: Create the concept and agree on the theme you will present to the prospective audience.

- Create a compelling name for the webinar or the webinar series. The name doesn't need to be extraordinary or clever, but it should clearly explain what the webinar is about and/or the value proposition.

- If you choose to create a series, create compelling titles for each webinar in the series.

- Create 100-word descriptions to be used widely in the promotion of the webinar. Descriptions should include the value the attendees will realize from the webinar.

- You may or may not want to create a brand around the webinar. A separate brand could include a logo, colors, look and feel of the promotion and the webinar itself. Creating a new brand for the webinar series requires resources and extra time.

- Create uniformly branded templates for emails, registration materials, and webinar presentation materials.

Step 3: Identify the players. You will need this group to be willing, available, and committed.

- Appoint a webinar manager or chairperson to make sure everything comes together. The webinar manager will own the webinar checklist and make it all happen on time and with the expected quality. The webinar manager is the project manager.

- Identify potential speakers and solicit them to volunteer and commit to the webinar. You might also need to talk to their managers to make sure they will have support to participate as needed. The speakers must be subject matter experts. It is very important that the speakers have the authority to speak about the topic. If the company and the speaker are not real authorities on the selected subject, the firm will lose credibility with the target audience.

- Identify a moderator. A professional moderator can go a long way toward improving the quality of the event. The moderator makes the introduction, moderates the Q&A sessions, and makes sure the webinar flows evenly and on time. You may choose to use a co-presenter format instead of a moderator format, but one of the co-presenters must take on the responsibilities of a moderator. Regardless of the format you choose, it is strongly recommended to have at least two speakers because it makes for a much more interesting listening experience. Using just one speaker works for a very short webinar (less than fifteen minutes), but any longer will be boring with just one speaker.

- Ideally, the chat moderators should also be subject matter experts, but you could get by with chat moderators who are not experts. I suggest one chat moderator for each 500 registrants.

- Assign a member of the marketing team to be the promotion manager. The promotion manager owns the promotion of the webinar or webinar series. It is up to the promotion manager to ensure that the target audience is aware of the webinar and that as many as possible register and attend.

- Assign a member of the marketing team to be the post-webinar manager. Activity after the live broadcast is critical for converting registrants and attendees into the sales funnel and ultimately into more sales. This person is responsible for post-webinar activity and conversion of the attendees to sales. The post-webinar manager should be involved with all interactions involving the sales team.

Step 4: Acquire or identify the tools necessary to create, produce, promote, and broadcast the webinar.

- You must procure a proper webinar platform to execute a strong webinar project. Don't try to use your virtual meeting provider or Google Hangouts as the webinar platform. Use a tool designed for broadcasting a webinar. There are a lot of options out there with different price points and features. Some well-known providers include ReadyTalk, Adobe Connect, ON24,

WebEx, or GoToWebinar. They all have pros and cons that bear analysis before you make your choice.

- A marketing automation platform (MAP) is ideal for promoting, managing, and measuring your webinar. However, you can still produce a webinar without one of the MAP tools.
- If you do not have a MAP, you will need an email service provider for invitations, reminders, and follow-up emails. Some webinar platforms include email options.
- Depending on the interaction of the sales team, you may want to use your CRM as a means to manage leads and campaigns. If you are able to integrate your MAP to your CRM, you will be able to attribute sales opportunities to the webinar activities.

Step 5: Promote the webinar.

Promotion or lack thereof can make or break the success of your webinar. Promotion of the webinar should be accomplished via multiple inbound and outbound channels. All promotional activities must make it easy for someone to learn more about the webinar and presenters as well as make it easy to register. If it's not straightforward, intuitive, and easy, you will lose people during the registration process.

- Your internal email list will be your best channel for promotion. I recommend sending an invitation email two to three weeks ahead of the broadcast date. As mentioned above, a marketing automation platform is ideal for managing the process. It's okay to send two or even three invitation emails to each of the contacts in your database. The recipients will not see the email invitations as spam as long as the topic is relevant and useful. Give them something they can use.
- Consider sending a press release announcing the webinar series.
- If you have social media followers or contacts on the various channels, be sure to push out information on a regular basis to tell followers about the webinar series.

- Advertise in venues where your target audience resides. Industry associations are excellent places to advertise educational webinars.

- Make sure you don't forget your own web properties. Place ads on your home page and all other relevant pages your target audience visits.

- Engage your sales team to tell their customers, prospects, and contacts about the webinar. Provide them with a custom email signature. Make up an email template they can easily forward to their contacts. Ask them to promote the webinar on their personal social channels.

- Create a custom landing page where you will funnel all traffic. Again, as mentioned above, make it super easy for people to learn more about the content, topics, speakers, and how to register. The landing page should tell a curious visitor what they should expect to get out of the webinar, details about time and date, and speakers' credentials.

Step 6: Broadcast the live webinar.

Some organizations prefer to record the webinar only for on-demand viewing and not to broadcast it live. There are some vendors that offer a hybrid, where you record the webinar but promote it as a live event in which the presentation recording is played but the chat feature is live. A live broadcast usually performs better than on-demand viewing, simply because it is an event.

- Try to use at least two speakers. Two or more voices and personalities makes for a more interesting event and keeps listeners more engaged.

- Use the interactive features of the webinar platform such as polls, surveys, quizzes, questions, and the chat feature.

- I do not recommend opening phone lines (or VOIP) for live questions. The sound quality is just too unreliable.

- Be sure to send automatic reminders as the broadcast day approaches. I recommend sending three reminder emails: one at seven days, one day, and two hours prior to the broadcast.
- Don't be disappointed when everyone who registered does not attend. Typically, you will get 20 percent to 30 percent of the registrants to attend the live event. If you get 50 percent or more, that is an outstanding attendance rate.
- PRACTICE, PRACTICE, AND PRACTICE! The key to your speakers sounding natural and confident is to practice.

Step 7: Follow up with both attendees and those who registered but did not attend the live event.

Post webinar activity is where they webinar gold is mined. If you want to see good ROI from all your work, make sure you follow up with attendees and, especially, those who registered but were not able to attend.

- Send a follow-up email as soon as possible after the broadcast, but no later than twenty-four hours after the live broadcast. Send one email to the attendees and a different email to the registrants who did not attend. Both emails must include links to the recorded webinar and to the slide deck.
- Some companies contact each registrant via telephone after the webinar. It is a great practice to call each attendee, ask for feedback, and offer another related high-value asset.
- Another great practice is to offer the high-value asset via a separate email one week after the initial follow-up.
- If you are executing a webinar series, make sure everyone who registered for the prior webinar gets invited to the next one.
- The key to converting registrants and attendees into customers is to continue to engage them with high-value content.
- Make sure to have a debriefing meeting with all those involved with the production and broadcasting of the webinar. Show special appreciation for your speakers, as it is likely they have

volunteered to participate on top of their regular day job. Talk about lessons learned. Ask each person to offer ideas about what went well, what should be done differently, and what should not be repeated. Above all, let everyone know how much you appreciate their participation.

Final Step: Measure and report the results.

- Compare the results to your objectives and goals.
- Report return on investment if you were able to tie the webinar activity to opportunities.
- Report on revenue-based metrics such as new opportunities and influenced won opportunities.
- Shout your success from the hilltops! See Chapter 15 for more on this.
- Get ready for the next one!

Appendix 2 - Enewsletter and Blog Pilot Program

Step 1: Choose a theme and decide on a name.

Be sure both the name and the theme are aligned with the audience-facing mission statement. The name should be meaningful and memorable.

Step 2: Select the tools and template.

Procure the necessary email service provider or choose a marketing automation platform that is able to deliver the email with best practices for deliverability and reporting capabilities. Design a template that is in line with your branding requirements. Any template should include an ad strip along the side or at the bottom of the email template. The template must connect the value offering with the brand and allow a reader to easily contact the proper people in the company should they be ready to request more information about the offering.

Step 3: Create a schedule.

Build a production schedule you can meet on a regular basis for an extended length of time. This decision usually requires an assessment of resources that will be needed; i.e., can you get it done with internal resources or will you need to outsource the production and distribution? It is critically important to send your email on a regular and consistent cadence. If the distribution is erratic, your audience will not receive the email as well as if they know when to expect it. Agree on an editorial calendar that specifies the asset and the topic at least six months in advance.

Step 4: Create a subscription and promotion plan.

Make a launch plan and a promotion plan for the email enewsletter. I strongly recommend making your email opt-in only. Do not automatically subscribe everyone or even large portions of your database to the enewsletter. By making the enewsletter opt-in or subscription based, you will gain much stronger engagement, supporting the three tenets of the new way strategy: TOMA, credibility, and reciprocity. Invite the people in your target audience to subscribe. Use outbound promotion, inbound tactics, and promote it on your website. It is okay to send an email blast to your database inviting people to opt in, but do not automatically opt-in the entire database. Use the tools at your disposal such as your website, outbound promotions, sales team, email signatures, etc. A subscription center landing page is a good idea, especially if you plan to expand with more than one enewsletter.

Step 5: Create the blog.

Aligning a blog with the enewsletter is a great way to complement the enewsletter. Some people may prefer to subscribe to a blog via RSS feed, and others may prefer to get the newsletter via their email inbox. Offering both is a great idea if you have the resources to support it. I do not recommend starting a blog alone without an email enewsletter. The reason goes back to Chapter 19, where we discuss best chance tactics. A blog is slow to catch on, and it is difficult to track participant numbers on a blog. A blog that repurposes the enewsletter content is good for onsite search engine optimization too.

Step 6: Measure and report the results.

Measure your email results on a similar cadence to your email send frequency. Make note of standard email metrics such as open rate, click-through rate, click-to-open rate, delivery rate, and unsubscribe rate. Pay particular attention to trends. In most cases, if you choose your topic well, you will see a very strong opening with a declining trend over the first few months. This is natural, and the trend should level out and begin to improve after six months or so. Pay particular attention to the unsubscribe rate. An increasing trend in unsubscribes means your subscribers are not seeing value or their expectations are not aligned with the email you are delivering.

Appendix 3 - Marketing Automation

The decision to purchase a marketing automation platform/service (MAP) for your manufacturing marketing team is a big one. Not only is it a big decision because of the monetary investment, it's a big decision because of the typically large cultural change that may be necessary for your marketing team and your entire revenue-generating function to support such a broadly invasive tool.

There are many companies offering MAP services with price points from a couple hundred dollars a month to several thousand dollars per month. The price is usually driven by the size of the database, features, and support plans. One of the good things about these tools is that the pricing is usually posted on the vendors' websites for easy comparison.

Is it worth the investment?

When a B2B marketer contemplates purchasing, implementing and integrating a MAP into their modern marketing tool kit, the concept is usually proposed to management with a supporting business case. It's fairly easy to show how marketing automation should improve the efficiency of the marketing team and increase sales, but it is very difficult to execute a plan that achieves these results.

My premise begs the question, "Is MAP worth it?" And of course, the answer is "It depends." Your initial investment in marketing automation will likely cost between $5,000 and $40,000 per year. It's not a one-time purchase price, but an ongoing subscription. It's not hard to show a robust ROI on paper based on some rosy efficiency numbers. However, the danger in determining if MAP is worth the investment is that there are many hidden costs that don't show up in the aforementioned business case or in the brochures and websites of the MAP companies. Hidden costs may include:

- Staff man-hours spent on implementation and learning how to use the tool

- Complexity of implementation and complexity in the actual use of the tool can be a large opportunity cost not to mention the cost of man-hours. Vendor cost for setup and training
- Outsourced cost for maintenance and execution
- Opportunity cost (could your time and money be better spent on something else?)
- Internal time and energy cost, not to mention cost to reputation if the project fails to meet expectations

Suppose you submit to the annual expense and agree to absorb the hidden costs, what is the payback and are you capable of using the tool to realize a payback? I hear from marketing directors and managers who have purchased a MAP subscription, excited by the possibilities, but are unable to fully use the tool because of lack of leadership, expertise, or personnel. They usually end up using it as an email tool. It is a very expensive email tool.

On the flip side, those marketing organizations able to fully leverage a MAP show more effective revenue and profitability. Naturally, this begs the question inherent in any correlation: Does better performance lead to deeper use of MAP or does full use of MAP lead to better performance? I don't have the answer to that question.

One may think that everyone in manufacturing is using MAP and if you and your organization don't get on board, you'll be labeled a laggard and end up missing the rapid growth boat to your more adoptive competitors. This is not the reality of the manufacturing marketing landscape. According to the 2012 Marketing Sherpa B2B Marketing Benchmark Report, only 24 percent of B2B marketers are using marketing automation. The report further states that of those 24 percent, at best 53 percent have implemented core functions. Only 30 percent have fully implemented advanced functions such as reporting dashboards, lead management, nurturing, or lead scoring. Therefore, only 8 percent of B2B marketers are fully leveraging their MAP.

More recent data, from a 2014 study by SiriusDecisions as reported by AdvertisingAge, states that only 16 percent of North American B2B companies use marketing automation. This report shows a wide range of adoption rates as broken down by industry, with the highest rate of 65 percent with information technology companies and the lowest rates with health care, financial services, and manufacturing, all with adoption rates of less than 10 percent.

Could this be opportunity knocking for your firm to get a leg up on the competition with a shiny new MAP? Perhaps, but there are some strong indicators of success you can benchmark against to help determine if you and your organization have a good chance of being successful with a MAP. For the sake of this discussion, let's define success as an increased revenue growth rate as a result of a MAP.

Based on my six-plus years of experience with purchasing, implementing, and using various marketing automation platforms, these are some key success factors for marketing automation:

- Make sure your key stakeholders are on board and excited about what a MAP can do for them. Key stakeholders might vary with your organization, but should start the executive team: CEO, CFO, CMO, VP sales, etc., and their associated teams.
- Have at least a preliminary plan written down and share it. Note the "written down" part of this step. If the plan is in your head or someone else's head, be wary, because the details of any unwritten plan are usually absent.
- Own the owner. You need to have one person who owns the MAP and is responsible for its success. This person should be on your team and not nestled away in the IT department or the sales department. This is your champion and, ideally, he or she loves technology, is curious, fearless, innovative, creative, and has a thick skin (shouldn't all marketers have thick skins?). Reward this person for success! If you try to add the responsibility for the MAP onto the litany of other tools the webmaster or another marketing person owns, it will be very difficult to get any traction with your new MAP tool. It will

likely languish as a glorified email tool at best and as a forgotten resource costing you $2,000–$3,000 per month at worst. Do not rely solely on outsourcing for strategy and execution. Outsourcing is no doubt a highly valuable resource, and I encourage supplementing your MAP with outsourced or freelance help, but that cannot and should not replace an in-house MAP champion expert.

- You will need the expertise of an outside vendor, especially if you plan to integrate MAP into other systems in place such as your CRM. The expertise of outside vendors will speed up your implementation, help get your team up to speed much more quickly, and set a strong foundation for future efficient use.

- Communicate. Communicate. Communicate. Let your whole company know how this tool is contributing to the goals of the firm. Be careful not to report vanity metrics or metrics that seem to be bragging about yourself or the team. Talk about how a certain campaign increased sales, for example. Even better, highlight the success of one of the stakeholders because of his or her use of the tool. You cannot over communicate the success of the MAP. As marketers, you might treat it as an internal product launch with a positioning statement, value proposition, and associated messaging.

- Measure everything and customize the presentation of results to fit the respective audiences.

Your team should be excited and interested to learn as much about this tool as possible. Every marketer should be assigned the task of becoming an expert in the MAP strategy and technology. Your team should plan to use this tool on a daily basis. Without that kind of interest, your success will be limited. If you plan to assign everything about the tool to one individual or a very small team of so-called digital marketers, your success will also be limited.

Is marketing automation worth it? No, if you're strapped for resources and won't be able to invest the time and absorb the hidden costs that are incurred to optimize the MAP. No, if your culture is not eager and ready for a marketing automation tool. Yes, definitely, if you are able to leverage the power and implement all the core functions to your marketing plan around an energized, technically savvy group of marketers.

About the Author

Bruce McDuffee

Bruce McDuffee has been on the ground in manufacturing marketing and sales for the past twenty years. He has been a field sales person, a global marketing director, and is now an independent consultant focusing on helping manufacturing organizations get their growth on with modern marketing strategy, tactics, tools, and teams. Bruce has been where you are now. He's had his share of ups and downs with the challenges of manufacturing marketing. He's been successful in converting the strong product culture to one of helping customers to be better. He is practiced at transforming the marketing function from a service center to sales and product into a valued and strategic contributor able to make a difference with audience engagement and proving contribution to revenue. Marketing for manufacturers is difficult, but it can be extremely rewarding. As founder and executive director of the Manufacturing Marketing Institute, he is striving to advance the practice of marketing throughout the manufacturing industry.

Technically, Bruce is a professional and progressive marketer who specializes in content marketing implementation and execution. Bruce has more than twenty-three years of marketing and sales experience in a wide range of business situations from start-up to global enterprise. His experience includes field sales, graphic design, marketing execution, and marketing production. He is a proven expert in driving growth with a combination of marketing automation and content marketing. Bruce is a super-user and administrator on the Eloqua platform and a Certified Marketo Expert. An MBA graduate from Northeastern University specializing in marketing and international management, he is an astute business professional. This powerful combination of modern marketing and business acumen has proven highly successful in leveraging the modern tools, strategies, and tactics best-in-class companies use to gain market share and boost growth rates at manufacturing companies.

Fresh out of college, Bruce was commissioned in the United States Navy, serving as a division officer in the Engineering and Operations Departments aboard USS Brewton stationed at Pearl Harbor. Following his tour in the Navy, he moved into the business world, where a passion for sales and marketing took hold.

In the past six years, content marketing has been his passion. As the global marketing director for a multinational electronics manufacturing company, Bruce was able to grow his business division by 11 percent, 19 percent, and 32 percent in subsequent years through applying a content marketing strategy in combination with marketing automation.

Bruce lives in Colorado with his wife and children. He enjoys road biking and photography outside the office.

Made in the USA
Charleston, SC
19 September 2016